CURIOU CHESTER

Portrait of an English city over two thousand years

TEXT, GRAPHICS AND PUBLICATION BY

GORDON EMERY
27 GLADSTONE ROAD
CHESTER   CH1 4BZ

©1999

PHOTOGRAPHS BY

MIKE PENNEY
LRPS

©1999

PHOTOS HAND PRINTED BY

JOHN MORGAN

PRINTED BY   **MFP DESIGN & PRINT**
Stretford, Manchester, M32 0JT

Printed on ZANDERS Mega Matt
produced from 50% recycled fibre and 10% minimum de-inked recycled.

credits

Thanks to the staff of Chester Record Office, Chester Library and Kall Kwik; Eileen Willshaw (Chester City Council), Dan Robinson (Grosvenor Museum) and Nic Fry (Chester Cathedral). Information was also supplied by Geoff Crump, Len Morgan, Roy Wilding, Michael Hoddinott, Mrs Foster, Terry Kavanagh and the late Ken Poole. Mayor Richard Short, David Maguire, David Mitchell and my daughter Cara posed for photos as well as customers at The Boot Inn. Premises photographed included those of The Falcon, Jigsaw, Worden Opticians, The Boot Inn, Pied Bull, Spud-U-Like, The Rather Nice Card Shop, Bull and Stirrup, Sofa Workshop, Telford's Warehouse and the English Speaking Union. Chris Erskine and Billy Fielder supplied the collectables, Fiona Richards the models and Colin Smith Chester silver. Thanks to all not mentioned here who have helped.

'Mercers' Row' is now known by the plain name: Bridge Street Row East

Lowe's shopfront is one of the oldest in the city

cover

Front: Chester Cathedral (before the reformed Garden of Remembrance - see page 232)

 A painting by Alex Campbell, Wern Mill Gallery, Melin y Wern, near Mold.

 Stone boss from the Church of St John the Baptist (p20)

Rear (top left to bottom right): Eastgate Clock (p206); Roman Gardens (p10); Bluecoat boy (p133); Ravens have nested in the city centre since 1997, the first in a city centre since medieval times; Sign on Old King's Head PH; Giant and pillar (p77 & p151); Devils (p68 & p77); Hugh Lupus crest on Queen's Park Bridge (p26 & p223); Fire sign, Lower Bridge Street (p227); Sealed Knot reenact the Battle of Rowton Moor (p108).

curiouser...

Look around the City of Chester and you will find few statues of local heroes. Apart from a military man (see page 186) who had tenuous links, and a marquis who had the city in his pocket (see page 187) there only a few statuettes of Chester's earls and a few funeral effigies paid for by some of the richest families. The most central statue in the city is a faceless abstract.

'A Celebration of Chester':
Stephen Broadbent's sculpture
represents thanksgiving,
protection and industry.

To find a famous person born in the city is difficult. Randolph Caldecott, illustrator, cartoonist and artist, is remembered by a blue plaque on Bridge Street Row West but LTC Rolt, who promoted Inland Cruising as a pastime, is nowhere to be seen. A roll of honour in the cathedral remembers the city's wartime dead, while lists of mayors can be found in several history books. But even the most outstanding mayors were merely figureheads, voted in and voted out by the Assembly or council, a body which, at first, was made up of the guildsmen or businessmen of the city. Individuality was not encouraged.

Even the unique rows of the city cannot be ascribed to one person. It is only later in the city's history that some credit is given to a few outstanding architects who have made Chester's buildings what they are today. When historians quote from names of fame it is usually visitors not residents that are mentioned, such as Wesley, Boswell, Defoe or Borrow. So it is unashamedly that I dedicate this book to those unsung heroes - the historians of the city who inscribed, copied, collected, transcribed and recorded Chester's life. From the scribes of Domesday to the monks Lucian, Vitalis, Higden and Bradshaw; from King and Ormerod to Hughes, Simpson, Bennet, Earwaker and Morris. There may not be statues in the streets for them but, for those who look, their words still occasionally shine from the annals, breviaries, books, papers and notes that they left behind.

...and curiouser

Historians recorded that, in Chester during 1437, the poor made bread from 'peas, feathers and fern roots'. Whilst one could imagine making pea bread or even mashing the tender shoots of ferns before they become poisonous — to eat feathers is beyond comprehension. However, studying the original entry for the annal suggests that the poor ate bread of 'peas, vetches and ferns'. Vetches are wild peas. Vetches are also the flights of arrows made from feathers. It would appear that the first historian who made this small error knew more about archery than wild flowers.

Although this volume does not pretend to be a full account of Chester's history or oddities, it is hoped that it will interest the reader and, although it is based on the history of this city, people from other areas will find reflections of their own cities, and glimpses of English history. Visions of the past are incorporated in the features of the present, and some of these will extrapolate into the future. Two thousand years have left indelible marks on the city of Chester. The former Roman fortress of Deva was named after the sacred Celtic river that has given its lifeblood to generations: transport to the Romans, defence and peace to the Saxons, power to the Normans, trade to the Elizabethans and tourism to the Victorians, continuing to the present day; food to generations, sport to the fit and drinking water to all.

Chester shown on 'Totius Britannae Tabula Chorographica' c1480. Harley MS 1808. To modern eyes there is something a little strange about this map with its south to north orientation.

Most visitors to the city see the sights, the wall and the cathedral, the rows and the riverside. I hope this book will introduce visitors and remind residents of the continuing saga of this living walled city, its history and its follies. Here, in twentieth-century photographs is a link to the past. People from every century would, if they could, turn the pages and recognise some of the features. Some might look back, others look forward in wonder. Whatever time and place you come from, I hope you will enjoy this guide as much as the author and photographer have enjoyed bringing it to you.

'Chester has many Curiosities'

SAMUEL JOHNSON 1774

CHRONICLE OF CHESTER

BC 55 [Julius Caesar's abortive
expedition to Britain.]

BC 54 [Julius Caesar invades
Britain with 5 legions, reaches
the Thames but returns to Gaul.]

AD 40 [Caligula assembles the
legions, apparently for invasion,
but then tells his soldiers
to collect seashells!]

AD 43 [Romans invade Britain
under Claudius.]

48 [Ostorius Scapula leads
expedition into Deceanglian
territory (North Wales).]

Top: An antefix (roof end tile) of the
20th Legion at DEVA (Chester).

[ ] indicates events outside Chester.

DEVA

The mighty legions fought the fierce Ordovician tribe of western Albion in Brittania. To attack the Island of Mond* the soldiers built flat boats to cross the strait. The cavalry rode or swam with their horses. On reaching the far bank they found, interspersed with the men, women dressed in black 'like Furies' holding torches, and the Druids chanting and cursing. The soldiers were stunned but were urged forward by their commander and slaughtered the barbarians.

Suetonius Paullinus returned east and south to reestablish control in the southern kingdoms where the warrior queen Boudicca of the Iceni had rampaged, killed and destroyed. The rebuilding of Londinium soon began. The second legion Adiutrix Pia Fidelis – loyal and true, marched northwest and found a perfect topographical position for their western port. Here they could import supplies, export lead and slaves while they planned the subjugation of 'Ierne', the other great island of Brittania. High on a sandstone bluff above the marshes, free from the floods of winter and everchanging shorelines of the estuary, where the rocky outcrops nearly touched across the river — an ideal ford or bridging point, at the mouth of the sacred Celtic river Dyfrdwy in the territory of the Cornovii, the legion appeased the holy waters by naming their wooden fortress DEVA.

*Ynys Mon/Anglesey

Shrine to Minerva with her owl in Edgar's Field near the Dee crossing. The cave beside may have been used by a Mithraic cult, with its baptisms and sacraments of wine and bread, which appealed to soldiers on the far flung borders of the empire.

Constantine suppressed the cult when he became a Christian.

Opposite: Deva's graveyard, an imaginative scene at the Grosvenor Museum backed by local artist Gregory Macmillan.

AD c50 [Gauls teach Romans how to use soap.]
c52 [Londinium founded.]
58-60 [Governor Suetonius Paullinus attacks Ordovices (west Wales) and invades Anglesey, wipes out Druids.] He may have built a supply camp at Chester.
61 Twentieth (XX) 'Valeria' Legion named 'Victrix' after victory over Boudicca.
63 [London rebuilt. A quay included infill of Roman armour, coins and a leather bag of hemp seeds. (Lond. Arch. Vol.8.2.)]
c70 [Legion II Adiutrix Pia Fidelis (loyal and true to Vespasian) posted to Britain.]

The bulging Roman north wall from Northgate Bridge

WALL

Valeria Victrix – brave and victorius over Boudicca, the 20th legion took over the fortress when the 2nd legion left to defend the frontiers on the Rhine and Danube. The momentous task of rebuilding in stone against the former turf embankments began. Beside the river crossing a shrine was dedicated to Minerva, the patron of all rivers and springs in Brittania. In Bath she had been linked with the Celtic goddess Sulis. She was fast becoming the most popular deity, representing soldiers, crafts and wisdom. Also known as Pallas and Athena, she was worshipped in the five day March Festival of Quinquatrix in Rome, where oblations, gladiatorial contests and a parade took place.

'(Built by) the century of Ocratius Maximus, in the first cohort.' COH:I:C:OCRATI:MAXIMI:L:M:P LMP may be the initials of the stonemason or a reference to a thousand yards.

8

Inscribed stones marked the sections of Deva's walls built by each century and as the walls grew so did the buildings both inside and outside the fortress. The interior was based on the customary four gates and streets within the rectangle. At the centre the principia or legionary headquarters included the strongroom. Across the street to the east was the legate's palace and to the west the barracks of the first cohort. Across to the south stood the scamnum tribunorum: officers' houses. The complex of hot baths, cold dips and exercise rooms was south of that, as were more barracks for troops.

Altars to the genii of men, their homes and the centuries of the legion were set up within the buildings. A princeps of the legion, Lucius Bruttius Praesens erected a shrine to Jupiter. Others raised shrines to Fortuna the Home-bringer, and other gods. Tombs had to be kept outside the fort and lined the roadsides with their inscriptions dedicated to the spirits of the departed.

Column bases in the principia.   Courtesy of Jigsaw, Northgate Street.

During 1821, in the cellar of 39 Bridge Street, 33 stone pillars of a 'hypocaust' were found. Each was 84 cm. high, supporting large square perforated tiles which had conveyed heat to the 'sudatorium' (sweating room) above. Twenty-eight pillars remain.

ON VIEW
ROMAN
BATH
AND
HYPOCAUST
Which is in a Perfect State of Preservation
AND
IN ITS ORIGINAL SITUATION

THE BATH
was built about the end of the
First Century and is therefore
OVER 1,800 YEARS OLD

AMPHITHEATRE

On the rebuilding of the amphitheatre in stone, or perhaps later, the centurion Sextus Marcianus, after a vision, had an altar to Nemesis, goddess of retribution and justice, set up by the north door. During the execution of criminals, after the animal fights and before the gladatorial battles, this would serve to remind soldiers and citizens that the law of Rome, carried out by men, was based on divine rulings. Afterwards Nemesis would transport the souls of the guilty to Tartarus.

Shrine from the amphitheatre

Order was the rule of the day and soon the natives were using Roman coin in their bartering and sending their sons to learn the Roman language, count in their numbers, protect the empire, build roads and cities, and eventually themselves become free Roman citizens.

Their daughters, although unable to marry soldiers, would receive their protection and favour, and in time bear their Romano-British offspring. Pax Romana!

Tile found in Chester showing a retiarius (gladiator with trident and net).

AD 74 II Legion under Governor Frontinus probably built the fort at DEVA (Chester). Lead pigs from N.Wales brought here.
80 [At Titus' inauguration an average 90 animals a day are slaughtered for 100 days at the Coliseum in Rome.]
86 II Legion posted to Danube. XX Legion takes over DEVA. Population estimate: 10,000
c102 Stone fortress started. Amphitheatre rebuilt in stone.
122 [Hadrian's Wall started in Scotland with XX Legion.]
141 [Antonine Wall started in Scotland.]
163 [Wall building in Scotland abandoned.]

Translation of discharge certificate:

"Emperor Caesar Nerva Trajan Augustus, conqueror of Germany and Dacia, son of the deified Nerva, Great Priest, in the seventh year of his Tribunician Power, four times saluted Imperator, Father of his Country, five times Consul, to the cavalry and infantry who are serving in the four squadrons and eleven cohorts named: First Thracian (Turkey), First Pannonian Tampiana (Hungary), Sebosius' Gauls (France), Vettonian Spaniards Roman Citizens (Spain), First Spanish (Spain), Vangiones 1,000 strong (Bavaria), First Alpines (Switzerland), First Morinarians (Belgium), First Cogernorians (Rhine), First Bactasiorians (Rhine Estuary), First Tungorians 1,000 strong (Belgium), Second Thracians (Turkey), Third Bracari (NW Spain), Third Lingones (Germany), Fourth Dalmations (Yugoslavia), who are in Britain under Lucius Neratius Marcellus, and have served for 25 or more years each and whose names are appended, has granted citizenship for them, their children and heirs, together with the right of legal marriage with the wives they had when citizenship was granted, or, if they were unmarried those they have subsequently married as long as it is only one.

January 19th, in the second consulship of Manius Laberius Maximus and Quintus Glitius Atilius Agricola.

For the Decurion Reburrus, son of Severus, from Spain, in the First Squadron Pannonian Tampiana commanded by Gaius Valerius Celsus.

Copied from and compared with the bronze tablet affixed in Rome to the wall behind the temple of the deified Augustus near [the statue of] Minerva.

(Witnessed by) Quintus Pompeius Homerus, Gaius Fabius Esubes, Titus Flavius Secundus, Publius Caulus Vitalis, Gaius Vettiennus Modestus, Publius Atinius Hedonicus, Tiberius Claudius Menander.

163 XX Legion rebuild DEVA
c200+ Itinerary of Antoninus gives distance, in Roman miles, to BOVIVM (Holt) XX, MEDIOLANO (Whitchurch) XII, RVTINIO (Bury Walls) XI, VRIKONIO (Wroxeter) XI.
213 [Constitutio Antoniniana (Roman citizenship to all).]
213-222 XX Legion titled 'Antoniniana'.
287 [Carausis claims to be Emperor of Britain] Last record of XX Legion on coinage of Carausis.
383-8 [Magnus Maximus proclaims as Emperor and attacks Gaul and Spain, kills Emperor Gratian but is killed himself.]

FROM OTHER LANDS

A bronze discharge certificate found in nearby Malpas dates to AD103. The retired troop leader from Spain had led a group who would now be called Hungarians. The Romans brought with them a multitude of soldiers and civilians from across the empire. Some of these retired here while some Britons recruited here retired abroad.

Discharge certificate of 'Decurioni Reburro'.

"Doctor Antiochus honours the best saviours of men among the immortals: Asclepius of the gentle hands, Hygeia and Panakeia."

This, one of two Greek doctors' inscriptions in Deva, dates from the end of the second century and echoes the Hippocratic oath. Doctors were treated as officers without fatigues in the Roman army but the two may have been military men or civilians. Asclepius was the Greek god of healing and medicine, Hygeia his daughter, goddess of health, and Panacea, another daughter was also a goddess of health able to 'heal-all'.

402 [Imports of new coinage into Britain cease.]
408 [Saxons attack (England).]
418 ['the Romans collected all the treasures in Britain and hid some in the earth and took some with them to Gaul'.]
429 [St Germanus visits Britain. 'Hallelujah' victory over Picts (at Mold).]
c475 Arthur fights his ninth battle at the 'city of the legions' (may have been Chester or Caerleon).
c603 St Augustine meets Celtic bishops at the city of the legions 'Legeceaster' (Chester).

The site of the Battle of Chester is unknown. Anglo-Saxon Chronicles record it around 609AD, two centuries after the Roman legions left.

The meadows (Earl's Eye or Earles Eyes in a deed of 1588 held at the Public Record Office, Kew) were given to the city by Mayor Harry Brown and Chester's first lady Mayor (1938) Mrs Phyllis Brown, owners of Browns of Chester.

A mythical beast with a scarlet eye in a green enamel body is a unique example of Romano-British art on the lid of a seal box (used to hold wax impressions) found under the present Odeon Cinema in Northgate Street.

Legeceaster

Who ruled Britain now? With the legions gone and no support from the empire, the Picts and Scots were driven off by Cunedda. It is written that Arthur tried to unite Britain, his name The Bear in both Welsh (Celtic) and Latin, fighting his ninth battle at 'the city of the legions'. *

St Augustine came to the city of the legions, but to try and unite the church and hold his synod with the Celtic bishops. A few years later, at the Battle of Chester, the pagan Ethelfrith, king of Northumbria, slaughtered many of the Celtic monks from the nearby monastery at Bangor Iscoed for taking sides with his Mercian enemies by praying and chanting for them. Saxon tribes, originally invited to protect coastal settlements, spread across England. Some slaughtered the local population but most lived, died and were buried beside them, their mixed race children once more adding to the gene pool of the nation.

Two and a half centuries later, when the Danes took refuge in the city, it may have been sparsely populated. King Alfred seized all the cattle, and laid waste the surrounding land to drive them out.

The next king and his queen, Alfred's daughter, Ethelfledd, started to rebuild. Now a Saxon 'burh', the walls may have been extended south and west to the river to enlarge the city. Wooden houses stood among the rubble of the former fortress.

No doubt trade was carried out with the Scandinavians. The first stone house recorded in the city in 1208 was bought from John Gunde and Agnes Outhcarle. It stood on the site of the present Old King's Head opposite the Church of Saint Olave. (King Olave of Norway was killed in 1070).

*Caerleon 'city of legions' is also the name of a fort in Wales. Legeceaster is the Saxon name for Chester.

c613 Battle of Chester: Ethelfrith, King of Northumbria, defeats Welsh and slays 200 monks from nearby Bangor Iscoed for praying for the enemy.
648 [Oldest illuminated manuscript with Romano-British ornament still remaining, dates from this year.]
660 Church and nunnery dedicated to saints Peter and Paul founded by King Wulphere (657-674) founded on present cathedral site.
689 St John's Church founded by King Ethelred (Giraldus).
690 Waerburh (St Werburgh, Wulphere's daughter) dies.

15

The shrine of Saint Werburgh was smashed in the Reformation but reconstructed in 1876. It is one of seven similar shrines in Britain.

shrine

Wulfere, King of Mercia, had a daughter named 'Waerburh' who became a nun at Ely and later took charge of the Mercian nunneries. In legend she was said to be so pure that when geese were found eating crops on the fields at Wedon in Northamptonshire she told her servant to instruct the geese to come and see her, which they did. She told them that they must all fly away and not return. The flock took off but continued to fly around in circles complaining loudly when they realised that one of their number was missing. Waerburh questioned her servant and found that he had killed one of the birds for the pot whereupon she miraculously brought the bird back to life from its bones.

Saint Werburgh raising the goose, depicted on a medieval misericord at Chester Cathedral.

Two centuries later, in the Danish raids, her remains, now just dust, were brought in a casket to the church of St Peter and St Paul in Chester. Queen Ethelfleda rededicated the church as a nunnery to Saint Werburgh, while creating a new church of St Peter in the middle of the city.

Even her dust was said to have miraculous properties. At the attack by King Gruffydd of Wales, her remains were carried to the walls and 'struck the King blind' so that he retreated. The Saint's remains were put in a shrine decorated with 34 Mercian princes and princesses.

Saint Werburgh's became a minster of secular priests under Earl Leofric of Mercia. A monk, Henry Bradshaw, at the later Benedictine Abbey wrote 'The Life of Saint Werburgh' in verse. It was first printed in 1521.

757 [King Offa of Mercia mints coin for overseas trade.]
c782 [Offa builds his dyke (earth wall) on the Welsh border.]
c796 St Bridget's Church in Chester founded by King Offa.
830 Hardyng's Chronicle claims: 'Aethelwolfe was kyn crowned at his citee Of West-Chester in all royal estate To who the Kynges and lordes made feaute And homage leege was preordinate
851 [Crossbows used in France.]
894 King Alfred besieges Danes in Chester. His army seizes all the local cattle, burns the corn, and his horses eat the area bare.

EDGAR the PACIFIC BEING ROWED DOWN THE RIVER DEE BY EIGHT TRIBUTARY PRINCES

King Edgar depicted on tile at the Bull & Stirrup P.H. in Northgate Street.

peace

Kynge Edgar approached the cite of legions
Nawe called Chestre, specified afore,
Where VIII kynges melt of divers nacions
Redy to give Edgare reverence and honour
Legiance and fidelite depely sworne full sore
At the same cite: after to be obedient
Promyt at his calling to come to his parliament.

From the Castell he went to the water of the Dee
By a prive posturne through walls of the towne
The kynge toke his barge with mycle rialte
Rowyng upwarde to the churche of Saynt John
The forsayd VIII kynges with him went alone
Kynge Edgar kept the storne; as most principall
Eche prince had an ore to labour withall.

Whan the Kynge had done his pylgrimage
And to the holy roode made oblacion
They entred agayne into the said barge
Passynge to his place with great renowne
Then Edgare spake in praysyng of the crowne
All my successors may glad and joyful be
To have suche honoumage, honour and dignite.

                    Henry Bradshaw, monk

c900 St Werburgh's remains
    moved to St Peter's and St Paul's.
906-907 Ethelred and Ethelfledd
    (Alfred's daughter) rebuild St John's
    and rededicate St Peter's and St
    Paul's to St Werburgh.
912 Ethelfleda (now the widowed
    queen) repairs the city walls.
    Coins from around this date
    found under St John's Church.
971 'All the kings of Britain came
    to him (Edgar) on a single day
    and acknowledged his supremacy'.
The eight row Edgar up the Dee.
1000 [Chinese invent gunpowder.]
1069 William the Conqueror
    takes Chester – 205 houses
    destroyed.

Saint John the baptist

King Edgar, after his coronation at Bath, came to Chester.
He was rowed upriver by eight kings who swore fealty to him.
This allegiance was consecrated at the small riverside Church of St John the Baptist.

Three centuries before, King Ethelred had founded a church here after being
told in a dream that he should build where he saw a white hind.
After rebuilding Chester's walls in the tenth century, Queen Ethelfleda
may have founded the first stone building, leaving foundation coins
of the realm under the masonry.

Later Earl Leofric repaired and enlarged the church, and installed
secular priests. St John's Church became the Saxon Minster of West
Mercia. In the eleventh century the Normans extended the stonework
again. St John's became Chester Cathedral under Bishop Peter of Lichfield.
However at the beginning of the twelfth century the see was transferred
to Coventry. In the fictional chronicle of Brother Cadfael, Ellis Peters
captures the essence of the time when she writes, 'A marvel, ... that
any bishop had ever contrived to manage so huge a see as the original
bishopric of Mercia, successively shifting its base from Lichfield to
Chester, back again to Lichfield and now to Coventry in the effort
to remain in touch with as diverse a flock as ever a shepherd tended'.

The move left a Collegiate church known, during the 13th, 14th and 15th
centuries, as the Church of the Holy Cross and St John. In the late 14th
century Gruffydd ap Maredudd ap Dafydd wrote a long poem which
includes a description of the cross.

Forty Saxon coins of Edward the Elder (ruled 899 to 925) were found five metres
under the Church of St John the Baptist in 1862.

The unusual coffin in the walls of the ruins is said to have been set up by the Reverend Richardson in 1813. It had been brought by canal boat from Nantwich Church by the Rev. Wm Massey. Another claim is that Benjamin Carter, the Sexton, found the wooden coffin while grave digging. The eastern ruins once held Priory House where Thomas de Quincy, author of 'Confessions of an Opium Eater' lived as a child.

'To the court of Lleon Gawr (Lleon the Giant –
a former Welsh name for Chester probably
based on Caer Leon) in the season of
winter, a bright wave of the sea brought
an image of resplendent beauty ... It is the
one relic of believers, of Mary, of the dead
and the Living; the Cross... of Christ.'

After the Dissolution the enormous church
building was reduced in size leaving the
west end in ruins and this happened again
in the 16th century leaving the east end in
ruins. In 1581 Queen Elizabeth I granted
the fabric of the church to the parishioners but there was a catch — she
wanted the lead off the roof to make
shot for her troops.

During the Civil War the Parliamentarians made
a platform for snipers in the west tower.

The 19th century saw a large scale restoration
and the incorporation of the organ which
was brought from Westminster Abbey where
it had been used at the coronation of
Queen Victoria, but a disaster was due
to happen. On 15th April 1881 the western
tower gave way and two sides crashed
to the ground — the 'long drawn out rattle,'
mixed with a cacophonic clash of bells,
was heard throughout Chester.

In 1975, on the 900th anniversary of St
John's Church (rebuilding by Earl Leofric)
the Midsummer Show was revived.

See page 77 for the Midsummer Show.

A Saxon stone cross head
from St John's Church.

1069 Count Gherbod given the
city but he returns to
Flanders where he is captured.
1071 Hugh of Avranches becomes
Earl of Chester and swordbearer
of England. In 1305 he was
referred to as Hugo de Lou,
and is now commonly known
as Hugh Lupus after his
wolf standard.
1075 Chester Parliament held in
the castle with 12 barons.
St John's becomes Cathedral
under Bishop Peter.
1085 Cathedral see trans-
ferred to Coventry. No
cathedral in Chester
until 1541.

The collapsing west tower on Good Friday 1881
destroyed the Early English porch.

'Here Harold is dead'   Bayeux Tapestry

CONQVERED

It was not enough to conquer England, William of Normandy had to secure his right to rule with the largest, or longest, piece of propaganda ever made: the Bayeux Tapestry. Early in the scene Harold is shown pledging allegiance (and the crown of England) to William. The story then tells of the invasion after Harold was crowned in his stead. After some 70 metres of woven cloth is a gory picture of dying soldiers with the news that Harold is dead. Is he the one with a spear through his gut, an arrow in his eye, or was he felled by a sword slash?

Some historians tell a different story — how Harold had many wounds, lost his left eye with the stroke of an arrow and fled to Chester. Here he lived for a short time as a hermit in the Chapel of Saint James near St John's Church. When Harold died, the Earls of Mercia, Edwin and Morkar, who had withdrawn from Harold to take up better positions against the Normans, went to London. They sent their sister Algitha, Harold's wife, to Chester with Aldred, Archbishop of York, and men from London who wished to crown Edgar Adlyng king but 'the fear of William' caused them to change their plans and they went to William to pledge their loyalty and fidelity.

Half a century later the Norman writer, Ordericus Vitalis, said that William carried out a 'barbarous homicide' in the harrying of the north. William reached Chester and the city finally gave way after 200 houses were destroyed. Vitalis claims that, on his deathbed, William reflected that he 'was bred to arms from childhood and was stained by the rivers of blood he had shed'. The Conqueror confessed about the English crown that he 'did not attain that high honour by hereditary right, but wrested it from the perjured... Harold, in a desperate battle'.

30th April 1782

To be Let or Sold with or without the Furniture a Small, well-finish'd House situate in St John's churchyard, in the city of Chester, called the Rock-House and consisting of a Hall, Dining Room and Bed Chamber...

The present 'Anchorite Cell' or hermitage near the site of St James' Chapel, below St John's Church, is a two-storey private residence. In 1611 it was called the 'Ankers Chapel'.

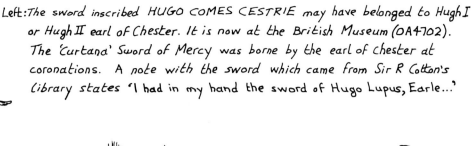

Left: The sword inscribed HUGO COMES CESTRIE may have belonged to Hugh I or Hugh II earl of Chester. It is now at the British Museum (OA4702). The 'Curtana' Sword of Mercy was borne by the earl of Chester at coronations. A note with the sword which came from Sir R Cotton's library states 'I had in my hand the sword of Hugo Lupus, Earle...'

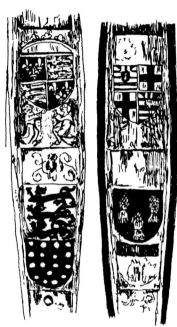

Above and right:
The enormous double-handed sword, bearing the arms of Edward, Prince of Wales and Earl of Chester may date from c1471 for the son of Edward IV. Prince Edward came to Chester 'in great pompe' during 1475. It bears six coats of arms for his six titles: the Royal Arms, the Prince of Wales plumes, the Duchy of Cornwall, Mortimer quartering de Burgh for the Earldom of March, Richard de Clare for the Earldom of Pembroke, and Blundeville's sheafs for Chester.

Now on display at the British Museum (SL17537)

26

RVLED BY SWORD

After the conquest, William gave England to his trusted earls and barons creating feudal fiefdoms out of relatively democratic Saxon townships. A Fleming, Gherbod was given Chester but left to fight in Flanders and was captured by his enemies. Hugo de Avranches, William's cousin became earl and held the county of Chester 'as freely by the sword as the king held England by the crown'. Although he also served as swordbearer to the king, Hugo or Hugh had his own parliament with his own barons. As well as Chester, he held land in 19 other counties as well as Normandy. The historian Orderic Vitalis states that 'he went about surrounded by an army instead of a household' and 'kept no accounts' and that 'his hunting was a daily devastation of his lands'. Ruthless he may have been but he also 'feared' God. He founded a new Benedictine abbey in 1093 at St Werbugh's and it is said that he entered the abbey as a monk shortly before his death, however even this is called into question by the Welsh, who called him Hugh Vras (Hugh the Fat). A plaque on the wall of Gwrych Castle in North Wales claimed that Hugh was killed there in 1100 whilst attacking Anglesey.

Chester's earls were a law to themselves. Earl Ranulph II even helped capture King Stephen in 1140, and ended up controlling a third of England after supporting Henry II's claim to the throne. The earldom eventually reverted to the Crown but was still ruled as a separate state in many respects. In 1398 Richard II confirmed that 'the said county of Chester shall be the principality of Chester'.

Because Chester's County Palantine was ruled as a separate entity from the rest of the country it also had its own laws. Outlaws from other parts of the country took advantage of this so that, in 1449, William, Bishop of Coventry and Lichfield petititioned King Henry VI to extradite

Seal of Ranulph (Blundeville)
earl of Chester 1180–1232.
19th century sketch by T. Frith.

fugitives of justice who, by the custom of the county palantine took refuge in Chester: 'there are within the county of Chester many advowrers, fornicators and other misdoers against the laws of God.'

A year later it was the Chester residents who were petitioning the king for their rights to be considered: 'Most gracious, benign and merciful king. We your humble subjects and obedient liege people, the abbots priors and all the clergy, barons, knights, squires and all the commonality of your county palantine of Chester, meekly pray and beseech your highness. Whereas the said county is and has been a county palantine as well before the conquest of England as since, distinct and separate from your crown of England...'
Henry replied to say that all their rights were safe.

1086 Domesday Book records the laws of Chester and its value: £30. St Werburgh's has houses for a church warden and 12 canons. St John's has 7 canon's houses. If a fire started the person responsible was fined three pence and had to pay his neighbour two shillings.
1092 Weir built on the Dee for mills.
1093 Earl Hugh founds Benedictine Abbey of St Werburgh.
1101 Earl Hugh becomes a monk a few days before he dies. Richard becomes earl.
1115 Great fire.
1118 Great fire burns down St Michael's Monastery near Pepper Street.

GIVEN BY HAND

The erle gave the place many great fredoms
Within Chester cite which ben knowen of olde
With singular priviliges and auncient customs
Saynt Werburge fair with profites manyfolde
That no marchendise shulde be bought ne solde
Enduryng the faire days (in writyng as we fynde)
But afore thabbay gate to have and to holde
Wherefore to the monasterie be never unkynde

Henry Bradshaw

28

A hand or glove representing the King's peace or protection was a common symbol hung at fairs countrywide and dates to early Norman or Saxon times. The word fair comes from the Latin feria (holiday). Chester's hand dates from a grant of trade liberties by Earl Hugh II in 1159. It was hung up 14 days before each fair. At that time there were fairs at Michaelmas and Midsummer. After the fair ended the hand was taken down and the 'leavelookers' would clear all unauthorised traders from the city. By 1687 it is recorded that a glove to give notice of a fair was suspended from a pole outside the Pentice (early town hall leaning on St Peter's Church).

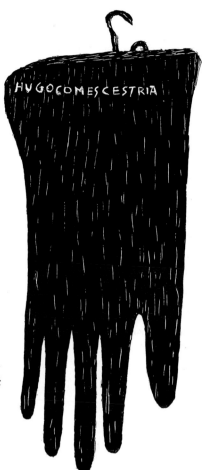

HUGO COMES CESTRIA
(Hugo earl of Chester)
Reverse: CIVIT. MERCAL
MCC IX (Guild Merchant
of the city 1159)

George Batenham's engraving shows the hand at St Peter's.

In the 19th century Peter Catherall the clerk was paid 3s9d a year to hang the hand from St Peter's Church. In October 1836, when he went to collect his fee, the mayor refused to pay for "such a foolish old custom" and told him he could do what he wanted with the object. The clerk did. He sold it or gave it to a Mr Wilkinson who, in turn, sold it for two pints of ale at the Sign of the Boot. On 27th December 1836 Joseph Butler bought it. After ending up at Liverpool Museum with the curious story of its travels attached, it was destroyed in World War II bombing raids.

ANCIENT BRIDGE

The Domesday Book of 1086 records how 'one man was sent from each hide [land area] to repair the bridge and walls. If he failed to come, his lord paid 40s'. In 1227 the bridge 'wasted away' and in 1279 a later bridge was washed away. It was replaced by a part-timber, part stone bridge in 1280. In 1357 the Mayor and Commonality were ordered to repair in stone 'as per the rest of the bridge'.

Old Dee Bridge

Traffic over the bridge was regulated by tolls, by ordinance (bye-law) and for defence. In 1241 the bridge keepers could take, for example, 'of every carte entringe with heringes, tenne herringes and of every horselode five ... And of every lode nuttes three handful'. In return the keepers had duties, 'to fynde lockes with keyes at twoe gates, that is to say at the gate of the bridge shipgate and at the horsegate [the horsegate or caplegate led to the river for watering horses] and one man allwais to keep the said gate of the bridge to shutt and open'.

The Mayor's Book for 1390 records a statute that 'No person having a cart with iron-bound wheels shall permit it to cross Dee Bridge on forfeiture of the cart and 6s8d to the king' but in 1533 Henry ap Res allowed carts with iron wheels to cross and was pardoned by the mayor.

In 1574 defensive measures on the bridge included 'in the middle thereof a gate of Iern which in the night was taken up'. A condition of sale for the southern part of the bridge in 1594 was that within three years there should be beautiful houses and buildings built upon it. The bridge was last widened in 1826 by Thomas Harrison but the downstream side kept its 'refuges' to protect pedestrians.

On the other side of the river lies Handbridge (Honebruge 13th century = stone or one bridge). Over the centuries frequent attacks on the area gave the village its Welsh nickname Treboeth (burnt town) although it was not always the Welsh that did the burning. In the Civil War a diarist records that 'Handbridge was made another treboeth being burnt by the command of the Governor Lord Byron to prevent their nesting others.'

Two-and-a-half centuries earlier, when Prince Henry (later Henry V) fought Owain Glyndŵr, he had arrived in Chester during 1403 and had the council issue a proclamation:

Toll fees, abolished in 1885 included 9d for a carriage, 2d a saddle horse.

'...we order that forthwith... you cause to be driven out without the walls of the city aforesaid all manner of Welshmen of either sex, male as well as female... and that no Welshman of whatsoever state or condition he may be, remain within the walls of the said city, nor enter into the same after sunset, under pain of cutting off his head: and that on no day whatsoever he journey or presume to go into the city with arms upon him ... except for one little knife for carving his dinner.'

Welshmen were not allowed in pubs or taverns nor to meet in groups of three or more. This bye-law, never repealed, has only recently been cancelled by the Race Relations Act but the proclamation had lost its effect, for in 1976 nine members of the Welsh Language Society took over the tax office and scattered papers about in a protest against 'the government's policy to encourage the decline of the Welsh Language'.

Tollgate Post, Handbridge.

OLDEST WEIR

The Romans may have had to haul their tiles and bricks made at Bovium (Holt) overland from Heronbridge because the river was not navigable all year but this was to change: 'The river of Dee was drawn unto the said cittie with great charge by the said Earle (Hugh) or some of his predecessors before the Conquest, from the Antiente course which it held before, a myle or two distant from the cittie, and a passage cut out of a rock under the walls of the said cittie.'

By altering the course of the river from Heronbridge, one fast flowing deep watercourse was created. The Earl's Eye(s) became meadowland, the defences of the city were enhanced and : 'The said earl (Hugh) also built the corn mills of Chester and erected the causey (weir) and granted three score fisheries above the said weir to several of his dependants, commonly called stalls in Dee reserving to himself the Earl's Poole, next to the causey and granted to the abbot the tithes of the said mills and fishings, which the dean and chapter have since enjoyed.' Harl MSS 2084.157

The weir was blamed throughout the centuries for the silting up of the river downstream but although Parliament issued an order to remove it in 1646 the City lacked the funds or will, and nothing was done. The mills of the Dee, on both sides of the river, carried on producing everything from flour and oatmeal to snuff and needlepoints well into the 19th century.

Then a new use was found for water power: the early 20th century Hydro-electricity Power Station was the first to serve an English city.

Opposite: In 1996 a narrowboat, Towy, trying to motor upriver at high tide, was caught on a log in the weir gate and then slipped sideways onto the weir. When the tide receded, the heavier stern went down with it, leaving the bow in the air. A log stanchion was propped under the bow to stop the hull breaking until the next high tide. Photo by the author.

Gilding on the tomb
of Godstall.

Godstall House

Godstall Lane: This lane
was also once known as
Bakers' Entry and was
the site of the medieval
St Giles' Bakery.

The lane has an even older
history — it ran alongside
the Praetorium or Legate's
Palace in the Roman
fortress of Deva.

Godstall

Did Henry V, Emperor of the Holy Roman Empire, King of Germany become a hermit and come to Chester in the 12th century?

Godstall or Godescal (warrior of God or called by God) had this narrow lane named after him. The red book or chronicle of St Werburgh's Abbey states that, in 1110, "*Henry (I of England) gave his daughter to Godescal, Emperor of Alemayne (Henry V, Holy Roman Emperor, King of Germany), who now lies in Chester.*" The historian monk, Higden, in the 14th century took this to mean that Godescal was buried here. In a list of street names compiled for Richard Dutton, Mayor, in 1567 it is stated that '*This godstall lieth Buried Within the abbay*'.

However, other historians claim that Henry V died in Utrecht with his wife, Henry I's daughter Matilda, present. Henry I of England also was not buried here in Chester, his remains lie in Reading. Matilda, after having been married to Henry V, thirty years older than her at the age of eight, was brought back to England and then married the Duke of Anjou, fifteen years younger than her, and bore Henry II of England. She eventually became a nun and was buried at Rouen. Some say it was Henry IV of Germany who became a Chester hermit but he died in Leige in 1106.

Then who lies in the rich alabaster tomb decorated with German eagles in gold leaf in the southeast chapel of the Cathedral Church of Christ and the Blessed Virgin Mary in Chester?

Tomb in the southeast chapel of the cathedral.

VNDERCROFT

The Norman undercrofts of the city were built as cellars to store and display much of the merchandise that came to Chester.

Built on the sandstone base rock under the city, these cellars were only underground at the rear where the collapsed Roman fortress rubble had raised the ground level. At the front they were only half underground with steps and small doors, sometimes under 1.5 metres high, from the street.

These unusual cellar shops became an integral part, and possibly a causal factor, in the formation of the medieval two-storey rows, unique to Chester.

The mid-13th century undercroft, vault or crypt at 12 Bridge St. was discovered under rubble in 1839. The upper building was rebuilt in 1664 by Thomas Cowper, mayor of Chester during the Civil War.

GUILDS

Earl Ranulph's charter to the guild merchants at the end of the 12th century assured them of the exclusive rights for retail sales within the city thus stabilising the economy. Henry III later confirmed these rights in his own charter which stated that 'No person whatsoever, not being free of the said city might or ought to sell or put to sale any wares or merchandise within the city or the liberties thereof...' This closed shop policy ensured good prices for Chester merchants.

Guildsmen had to be freemen of the city. They had to take an oath at the Pentice (the council chambers) to serve the city and the king. Rolls of Freemen were published to ensure that rogue traders or 'foreners' could not sell their wares, although foreigners could pay for the privilege at markets or the fairs. The 'leave-lookers' of the city collected a 'levy' or toll to sell from these unfree tradesmen.

During 1534, rules for the King's Fishboard, an open fishmarket in Watergate Street, were that all 'Salmon, Mylvell, rey or any other sea fish' were to be sold at the market. Citizens could buy before 9am, fishmongers had to wait until after, while 'foreign fishers' could only cut and retail after 10am. It was illegal to regrate (buy up stocks and sell on at inflated prices) or forestall (buy or sell before reaching the market). Sheriffs' Books show some of the penalties for offenders: 1505 'John Wright is a common regrator and forestaller of the market 3s4d'; 1507 'Geoffrey Ibid of Handbridge drover forestalled 10 hens, 12 geese and 80 eggs coming to market 4d'; 1511 Alice Chalerton continually forestalled the market bringing in victuals and coming to market before the proper hour 12d, Ralph Norton glazier for the like 8d.'

There were four ways to become a freeman and guild member: by apprentice-ship of five to seven years, by purchasing membership (in 1453 this was a fee of 26s8d), by being born free as the son of a freeman (for sons, dues in 1453 were remitted to a token 10½d), or by becoming an honorary freeman as a gift of the Assembly (city council).

One of several
charters held by
Chester Record Office
which show how
the City of Chester
gained a separate
identity for self
government.

Photo: Chester Record Office (CH5)

As well as running local government, the guilds took responsibility for the welfare of their members and their families. They took part in the Midsummer parades and the Mystery Plays. Guildsmen had to attend meetings and could not sue other guildsmen without informing the officers of the guild. They had their meetings at inns or in the towers on the city walls. No person of any 'arte, mystery, syence, occupation, or crafte' could 'intermeddle' or practice another trade. In the 15th century the Innkeepers threatened to brew their own ale but the Brewers took them to court and it was ordered that only the Brewers could brew.

Of 25 original guilds, 19 companies were recorded in 1475. Charters of incorporation were granted to each guild, the earliest to the Bakers in 1462. Although the Bakers were the only ones normally allowed to sell bread in the city they were also under strict rules. The mayor and Assembly fixed prices of bread, while gorse for the ovens had to be stacked outside the city walls. Nowadays this area of 'Gorse Stacks' is reserved for storing another item. It is a car park.

In 1533 another company was formed. This was the 'Merchant Venturers' or Meere Merchants who were the only traders allowed to merchandise in foreign parts and, at first, they were not allowed any manual trade or retail sales in the city.

On the 17th December 1694 it was ordered that 'No man shall have any Commerce Trade or Dealing wth any man that shall sett up Stale or Hake in the street of ye said Citie neither at the ffaire or market but to dispose of his goods at his shope or house he keeps all the yeare.' but this was the beginning of the end for the guilds' monopoly of city trade.

Opposite: Grant and confirmation by Ranulph, earl of Chester to the citizens of Chester of their Gild Merchant with all the liberties and free customs enjoyed by them in the time of his ancestors. c1192

1120 [White Ship sinks with Richard, earl and his brother Ottuel.] Randle Meschines (Ranulph I) becomes earl and chooses three wheat sheaves as his coat of arms. He converts the Wirral farmlands to a hunting forest. Population of Chester estimate 2,500

1121/9 Sheriff recorded.

1129 Ranulph II becomes earl.

1140 Earl Ranulph helps capture King Stephen at Lincoln. Fire in city.

1144 Robert of Chester writes 'Liber de Compositione Alchemiae'.

1146 Poulton Abbey founded by an officer of Ranulph II to pray for the health and safety of his liege lord (but see 1153).

c1147 Ranulph II founds Nunnery of St Mary.

Minstrels

Seal of Roger (de) Lacy

When Earl Ranulph Blundeville was besieged in Rhuddlan Castle during 1198, his constable Roger Lacy was sent to Chester to fetch help. On arriving in the city the constable found a 'tumultous Rout of Fidlers, Players, Cobblers and debauched persons, both men and women' who had come to the Midsummer Fair. He led all those he could muster back to Rhuddlan. At the sight of this enormous army the Welsh fled.

In thanks, Lacy was given authority over shoemakers and minstrels. This right devolved to his son John then to his steward Hugh de Dutton. A minstrel's court was held yearly on St John the Baptist Day, the first day of the Midsummer Fair, where the minstrels would swear allegiance and pay a fee (2^s2^d in 1642). As late as 1754 twenty-one licences were granted; the last court in 1756.

As well as licensed minstrels there were also city waits – musicians employed by the city. In 1591 the 'waitesmen of the said Citie' had 'instrumentes of musick viz the how boies the recorders the cornets and violens'. Occasionally the minstrels and the waits were in competition. In 1610 there was a fracas when two or three 'of Mr Dutton's men of dutton unto them and tooke the instruments from the musicke'. On other occasions both minstrels and waites were employed. In 1672 four waites were given livery every three years. At Christmas they were paid 10^s to play morning and evening in the city streets but were not allowed to leave the city without permission.

Opposite: Modern day minstrels and buskers are still encouraged to sing for their supper.

1153 Peverall, earl of Nottingham, poisons Earl Ranulph 'by witchcraft'. Hugh II becomes earl of Chester.

1173-77 [Earl Hugh imprisoned in Normandy, eventually ransomed.]

1180 First mention of Holy Trinity Church. A great fire is prevented by parading Saint Werburgh's remains through the streets.

1181 Ranulph III becomes earl.

1182 Robert of Chester translates 'De Astrolabio' from Arabic to Latin (Bodleian Library Cod Digb 162 f3).

1190 Earl Ranulph gives a charter to the citizens guild. St John's Hospital founded 'for the sustentation of poor and sillie persons'.

Each night the curfew bell is rung at 8-45pm and the gate closed at 9pm by a cathedral verger. The custom of curfew, which was practised in many English cities, dates back to the Norman law of Couvrefeu (cover Fire) when fires had to be covered or extinguished and citizens shut up safe inside their houses to protect the city at night.

CABBAGES and COLEWORTS.

Names. I shall spare a labour in writing a description of these, since almost every one that can but write at all may describe them from his own knowledge, they being generally so well known that descriptions are altogether needless.

Place. These are generally planted in gardens.

Time. Their flowering time is towards the middle or end of July, and the seed is ripe in August.

Government and virtues. The cabbage or coleworts boiled gently in broth, and eaten, do open the body, but the second decoction doth bind the body : the juice thereof drunk in wine, helpeth those that are bitten by an adder; and the decoction of the flowers bringeth down women's courses. Being taken with honey, it recovereth hoarseness or loss of voice; the often eating of them, well boiled, helpeth those that are entering into a consumption : the pulp of the middle ribs of colewort, boiled in almond milk, and made up into an electuary with honey, being taken often, is very profitable for those that are pursy or short-winded ; being boiled twice, and an old cock boiled in the broth, and drunk, helpeth the pains and obstructions of the liver and spleen, and the stone in the kidneys ; the juice boiled with honey, and dropped into the corner of the eyes, cleareth the sight, by consuming any film or cloud beginning to dim it : it also consumeth the canker growing therein. They are much commended being eaten before meat to keep one from surfeiting, as also from being drunk with too much wine, and quickly make a drunken man sober; for as they say, there is such an antipathy or enmity between the vine and the colewort, that the one will die where the other groweth. The decoction of coleworts taketh away the pains and achs, and allayeth the swellings of swoln or gouty legs and knees, wherein many gross and watery humours are fallen, the place being bathed therewith warm : it helpeth also old and filthy sores being bathed therewith, and healeth all small scabs, pushes, and wheals, that break out in the skin ; the ashes of colewort-stalk, mixed with old hog's grease, are very effectual to anoint the side of those that have had long pains therein, or any other place pained with melancholy and windy humours. Cabbages are extremely windy, whether you take them as meat or as medicine : but colewort-flowers are something more tolerable, and the wholesomer food of the two. The Moon challengeth the dominion of the herb.

Coleworts (Kale)
from 'Culpepers Complete Herbal'

kaleyard's gate

In 1274 the monks of St Werburgh's Abbey were given permission to have a gate in the city walls to reach their vegetable garden. However the 1323 Plea Rolls of the County Court show problems with gates: 'Dissentions having arisen between the Abbot and Convent of Chester and the Mayor and Commonality of the city, touching the closing of the postern of the said abbey, in the wall of the city contiguous to the abbey: it was covenanted that the said Abbot and Convent and their successors should hold the said postern closed in time of peace, on condition that they made a drawbridge across the ditch in the garden of the said abbey, and supported the said bridge, and took such measures for the security of the city as they should deem fit, by the custody of the keys, and drawing the said bridge: and that they destroyed the great gate erected by them in their own proper wall, and kept the place closed; in lieu of which the said Mayor and Commonality were to permit the said Abbot to make another postern in the place outside the walls of the convent in which the swine was accustomed to be, the said door to be of such dimensions that a man on foot might lead a horse through without difficulty, the same to be closed in time of war, should the safety of the city require it.'

By 1450 it appears that there were still two gates at the abbey but by 1509 just one. In 1584 the cathedral paid 2d for a new lock for the 'Cailliard Gate'.

During the Civil War, Sir William Brereton, attacking the city for Parliament, reported that, 'All the ports (gates) made up and strong guards sett upon some of them within pistoll shot soe that none remained open but one little salley porte which is betwixt the Phenix Tower and the Eastgate'.

The gate may have been rebuilt, as ashlar in the arches was dated 1693 RH (Randle Holmes).

1194 Lucian, monk, states Cheshire distinct in bounds, people and privileges 'and the virtues of its earls, Cheshire answers in its assemblies more to the sword of its prince than the crown of a king'.
1198 Earl Ranulph besieged at Rhuddlan. A host of players and minstrels from the Midsummer Fair march to Wales like an army, forcing his release.
1208 Peter the clerk buys a stone house (the first recorded in the city) from John Gunde and Agnes Outhcarle.
1218 Earl Ranulph joins Crusades.
1232 John, last independent earl.
1236 Black (Dominican) Friars come to city.
1237 Earldom reverted to the Crown under Henry III.

Pentice

The first record of the Pentice is from 1288 although the shops underneath may have been the shoeshops recorded ten years earlier. This structure which leaned against St Peter's southern wall was enlarged in 1573 and blocked most of the entrance to Northgate Street. It was Chester's first town hall and held the council chambers and the mayor's office.

Pentice, Pendice or Appentice from Appendere: to add or attach.

This drawing of the Pentice is based on a sketch by J. Turner drawn between 1783, when St Peter's Church spire was taken down, and 1803 when the Pentice was demolished. St Peter and St Paul's Church had first been sited where the Cathedral now stands but when St Werburgh's remains were brought to the city 'the olde churche of St Peter and of Paule... was translate to the myddes of the said cite, where a paresshe church was edified truele'. By the eleventh century the church was known as St Peter's 'templum'.

The Pentice Court held here by the sheriffs dealt with matters of debt and trespass (similar to today's County, small claims, Court) while more serious cases were held at the Portmote Court in front of the mayor (similar to today's Magistrates Court). The Crownmote Court was held in Chester Castle. (Today's Crown Court is held in the rebuilt castle.) An early record, the Pentice Cartulary, states that, 'In the Appentice the pleys which towche freeholde be non in eny wise pleadable butt in portmote nor ought in the pentice pleyse of covenannte which touch lannde rente or such other plays which touch anny tie or pleys or replevy suche to be pleaded.'

The year 1713 saw an order 'for preventing dangers that may happen by fire', made in 1709, 'writ fair and put into a frame and hung up in the pentice of this city.' Five years later, pictures of Owen Jones and John Lancaster, who set up city charities, were painted on the inner wall.

In 1781 Lord Grosvenor, the bishop, the members for the city and Sir Peter Cunliffe widened the Northgate Street by taking down the back pentice. The inner pentice was rebuilt to a plan by Joseph Turner. The windows were changed to sashes in 1794. In 1803 George Lowe, goldsmith, had the glove or hand for the fair above his shop but when the Pentice was demolished he moved his business to Bridge Street Row East. Thereafter the hand was hung from the corner of St Peter's Church.

"The Mayor remaineth most part of the day at a place called the Pentice, which is a brave place builded for the purpose, at the High Cross under St Peter's Church, and in the midst of the City, in such a sort, that a man may stand therein and see into the markets, or four streets of the city, there sit also, in a room adjoining, his clarks for his said Mayor's Courts, where all actions are entered and recognizances made and such like."

Daniel King 1651

1237 Grey (Franciscan) Friars in city.
1238 First recognised mayor, William the clerk.
1244 Two city sheriffs until 1835.
1245 Henry III allows Black Friars to take stone from the castle ditch to build their houses.
1251 King Henry III starts stone castle.
1254 Prince Edward (later Edward I) created earl of Chester.
1267 le lorimers' row mentioned.
1275 Monks put Kaleyard Gate in wall.
1277 Edward I marches from Chester on the Welsh at Rhuddlan Llewelyn defeated.
1278 White (Carmelite) Friars building friary. Great Fire.
1280 St Nicholas' Chapel built.

Medieval Rows

What were the origins of Chester's unique rows? Although the term has come to mean the first floor galleried walkways, this was not always the case and there are still ground floor rows remaining : Lorimers' Row (harness-makers) under the Bluebell, which dates back eight centuries, as well as St Werburgh's Row, built in 1935. Other cities had rows where certain similar tradesmen gathered. In 1634 it was ordered that all Goldsmiths in London were to be accommodated in Goldsmith's Row in Cheapside or Lombard Street.

Some of the oldest shops recorded in Chester were 'undecim seldas quae vocantur seldae sutorum in Bruggestrete' (eleven stalls called the shoemakers' shops in Bridgestreet). Th shops may have been under the Pentice or part of a row on Bridge Street. In 1356 a grant records 'a site in Brugge Street near the stairs leading towards Le Corvyserrowe at the end of the Fish Board near the pillory in the corner facing St Peter's Church'. This description gives a picture of the centre of the city. The King's Fishboard was the medieval fish market that survived in Watergate Street for over four centuries. A 'corvyser' was a cobbler but usually different than a shoemaker. 'Le Corvyserrowe' was on first floor level along Bridge Street West Row.

C19th engraving

The Linen Market was held in Watergate Street South Row in the C17th.

46

Under the Pentice at the top of Bridge Street and turning into Northgate Street as far as the steps to St Peter's churchyard was Pentice Row, a ground floor set of shops with no covered walkway. Cookes Row was another name for Pentice Row. There were also ironmongers in Pentice Row on Northgate Street suggesting that this may have been Ironmongers' Row which stretched up the west side of Northgate Street recorded in 1330 and 1550. This was replaced by, or continued into, Shoemakers' Row. On 23rd August 1616, King James I returned from the cathedral by way of Shoemakers' Row to banquet in the Pentice. This row was also once recorded as John Moyles' Row but this was probably just a nickname after a trader. Shoemakers' Row was demolished in Victorian times, partly to make way for Harrison's 'Commercial Newsroom' which still stands. According to Dodgson in 'Place Names of Cheshire' a Shoemakers' Row was recorded in Eastgate Street in 1651 (but this is doubtful). Having two or three Shoemakers' and

Boots hanging from the beams in Shoemakers' Row, Northgate Street (now demolished).

Corvisors' rows at different times has led to continued confusion amongst historians.

In 1278 there were 'Botersoppes' (buttershops) — the upper and lower shops in Northgate Street East and Eastgate Street North. The first floor of these in Northgate Street earned the name Broken Shin Row due to its poor surface. Saflerisrawe (Sadlers' Row) in 1343 was possibly in Whitefriars while 'le Flessherowe' existed as a butchers' first floor row by 1345 in Watergate Street North. In a deed of 1421 Robert le Vernon 'Taillour' was granted one shop under ' le Flesshenerrowe in Watergatestrete' while another deed in 1555 included the street level 'cellars' in the row.

Welsh Row, selling Welsh Flannel was low down Watergate Street. After the Civil War, in the 17th century, the Linen Market was held on Watergate Street Row but spread further leaving Thomas Bolland on Bridge Street Row West complaining that the resulting obstructions from the 'flax market' stopped customers reaching his shop. In actuality there have always been steps about every four shops apart.

In 1656 Daniel King stated: 'It is a goodly sight to see the number of fair Shops, that are in these Rowes of Mercers, Grocers, Drapers and Haberdashers, aspecially in the street called, The Mercers Row. Which street, with the Bridge street, (being all one street) reachith from the High Crosse to the Bridge, in length 380 paces of Geometry...'

Other records keep Mercers' Row from the Cross to Feathers Lane, followed by St Michael's Row (not the Edwardian one in the Precinct) to the church. In Lower Bridge Street names such as Rotten Row and Old Coach Row were given.

Dutch House(s) in Bridge Street West (Scotch Row or Ship Tavern Row) by G. Cuitt 1809.

Bridge Street West from the Cross to Commonhall Lane was known as Scotch Row in 1860, or sometimes Ship Tavern Row. From there to Pierpoint Lane was Flax Row. Beyond the lane was Bolland's Row after Thomas Bolland, sometimes known as Harp and Crown Row. Eastgate Street Row South was Cornmarket Row for many centuries with Talbot Row or Royal Hotel Row by the Grosvenor Hotel. 'Bakestris' or 'Baxter' Row was along Eastgate Street North Row, near the entrance to Godstall Lane (Bakers' Entry) and the medieval site of St Giles Bakehouse. Paradise Row and Bedward Row were just rows of houses to the west of the city.

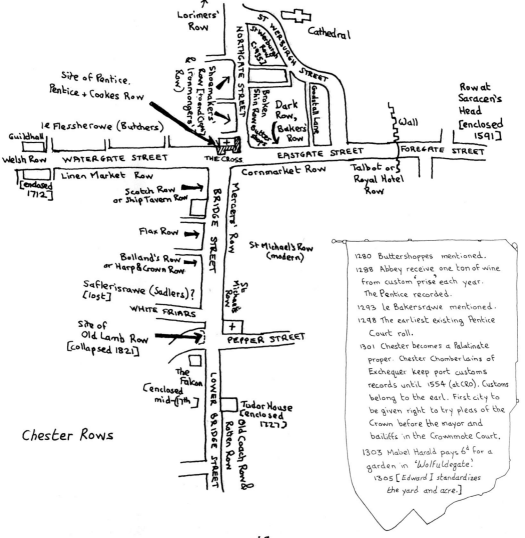

Chester Rows

1280 Buttershoppes mentioned.
1288 Abbey receive one ton of wine from custom 'prise' each year. The Pentice recorded.
1293 le Bakersrawe mentioned.
1298 The earliest existing Pentice Court roll.
1301 Chester becomes a Palatinate proper. Chester Chamberlains of Exchequer keep port customs records until 1554 (at CRO). Customs belong to the earl. First city to be given right to try pleas of the Crown before the mayor and bailiffs in the Crownmote Court.
1303 Mabel Harald pays 6d for a garden in 'Wolfuldegate'.
1305 [Edward I standardizes the yard and acre.]

So how did the galleried first floor rows come into existence? Were they based on Roman piazzas, with a natural progression from the stone vaults underneath? The vaults or cellars were certainly part of the cause but it was the wealthy medieval merchants who seem to have decided to fit their buildings into this unique arrangement. During 1277 Edward I's armies were in Chester preparing for their Welsh campaign. This large influx of people, together with the fact that much of the land within the city walls was in the hands of religious orders, must have increased pressure on the space available. A city fire on 15th May 1278 may even have paved the way for a new building programme. The king had brought with him hundreds of carpenters and stone masons and there were, no doubt, others looking for work in the most expensive castle-building period in Britain's history as Edward consolidated his conquest of Wales. Edward's engineer, Master Richard, well-used to planning castles and street layouts, became Mayor of Chester in 1305.

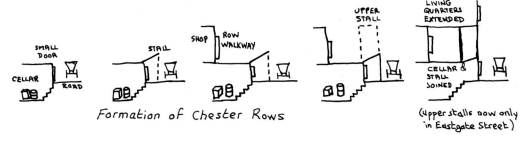

Formation of Chester Rows

(upper stalls now only in Eastgate Street)

With the cellars above the usual level because of bedrock, stalls were needed outside to sell wares. This, in turn, made entry difficult to top storeys so walkways and steps had to be built. At an early period it is clear that the council regarded these as public rights-of-way. By 1673 'all benches or showboards in the rows or streets' had to be 'made with hinges' so they could be 'folded up at night'.

There were once far more rows than those that remain. They even stretched into Foregate Street where, in 1591, permission was granted to enclose 'le rowe ad Saracen's Head' (numbers 41-45). During the Civil War, Sir Richard Grosvenor lived in his town house, now the Falcon, and it was 'too little to receive his family' so he had permission to enclose the row at the corner of Cuppin Street and Lower Bridge Street.

The row frontage in the Falcon can be seen dividing the front room.

In 1712 application was made to enclose 'a dangerous and useless row' at the far end of Watergate Street opposite Trinity Church while in 1717 another 'useless row' down the west side of Lower Bridge Street was enclosed. During 1727, for a payment of £5, William Bulkeley was granted permission to enclose the row on what is now Tudor House. The year 1729 saw the row at the Hope & Anchor (near the present Odeon) in Northgate Street enclosed. Only small portions of the first floor rows in Lower Bridge Street remain, many having been incorporated into the upper storeys of buildings, as in the Tudor House and the Falcon.

Some models of the Northgate Street West Row by Fiona Richards of Paper Clay Designs.

The historian, Frank Simpson, points out in his notes that Chester stalls were leant against buildings whereas in other market towns they were in the middle of the street. Were Chester tradesmen farsighted enough to realise that every shopping street could be doubled, or sometimes tripled, in size with upper and outer stalls? Over the years the shops encroached further and further into the street, leaving space to put up more stalls on the outside of the upper walkways and extend the solars or bedrooms above those. The council still kept a grip on the

Old Lamb Row from Hugh Roberts 'Chester Guide' 1851

Old Lamb Row, said to have been 'one of the most remarkable objects of curiosity in the city.' Built in 1655 it was ordered, in 1670, that 'the nuisance built by Randle Holme be taken down' but it remained. In 1821 the front of the upper compartments fell into the street. A woman, Sarah Adams, was inside and suddenly was in full view of the passers by. This accident saved the council some expenses when, a few years later, the new Grosvenor Street was laid through the site.

situation, its own future secure from the fines(rents) from encroachment and a strong commercial base — all aldermen also being freemen from the guilds. New buildings and alterations to the streets and rows had to be passed in Assembly. However, Eastgate Street North was packed with so many shops on the outside of its first floor row, blocking the light, that the passageway became known as Dark Row.

Celia Fiennes (1662-1741) who rode through the country on horseback described the rows as 'penthouses set on pillars'. Daniel Defoe thought the rows 'old and ugly', and in 1763, Elizabeth, Duchess of Northumberland wrote that 'The Rows in this City are both ugly and inconvenient.' Clearly these were just personal opinions for Wesley, in 1752, found them 'the greatest convenience', especially in the rain.

Seven hundred years after Chester formed its unique medieval row system, modern planners worldwide build their shopping centres, often with two floors and balconies, sheltered from the weather.

Chester's First-Floor galleried row tradition has been incorporated into the award winning design of Rufus Court in Northgate Street

53

Three Old Arches

1274AD   **1274AD**

Three Old Arches

Said to be the oldest stone shopfront in Britain, these arches may even date to the early 13th century. They start at street level. Behind them is a medieval parallel hall, the largest structure ever found in the rows. Building in stone may have saved the top storey from the many fires that ravaged the city. Unlike many other rows buildings this frontage has not been extended with stall boards over the street making it a unique example of a medieval row.

Until 1999 part of the store was a grocery. Compare typical grocery prices with this bill in 1559 for Margaret (or Market) Dingley (This may have been a household bill or she may have been a market trader buying wholesale.) Prices were in pounds (£) shillings (s) and pence (d), weights in pounds (lbs) and ounces (ozs).

Grocery Bill from Cheshire	£	s	d
Two Loaves of Sugar 20^{lbs}/0^{ozs}	1	4	11
Cinnamon Elect 1^{lb}		9	4
Damaske Promes (Prunes) 20^{lbs}		3	4
Malaga Ressins 10^{lbs}		1	8
Fine Carrants 6^{lbs}		2	6
Macs (Mace) Large 1^{lb}		14	0
Anisieds 2^{lbs}		2	0
Liccores, Tryed (they may have been tried but this means dried)			10
Cloves 8^{oz}		4	0
Saunders (Sandalwood) 8^{oz}		2	0
Torne foll (Castor Oil seeds) 4^{oz}			6
Comfitts, 1 box (probably caraway sweets)		1	6

PORT WATCH TOWER

The Domesday Book of 1086 records that, 'If ships arrived or departed from the port of the city without the king's licence, the king and earl had 40 shillings from each man who was on the ships. If the king's reeve* ordered those who had marten pelts not to sell to anyone until they had first been shown to him and he had bought, whoever neglected this paid a fine of 40 shillings'.

Chester's port was still flourishing in 1195 when a monk, Lucian, wrote:

'Chester has, beneath its walls, a beautiful river abounding with fish, with a harbour on its south side where ships from Aquitaine, Spain, Ireland and Germany unload their cargoes of wine and other merchandise'. In fact wine was only imported through four other English ports, London, Bristol, Sandwich and Southampton.

Wine was imported in hogsheads known as tuns (252 gallons). The earl had the rights to a 'prise' of all imports. One tun before the mast and one aft was taken off with a value of 20 shillings each. In 1302 the merchant vintners of Aquitaine obtained remission to pay a toll of two shillings per tun instead.

*The reeve was an accountant with legal powers. The shire reeve is more often known by his later name: the sheriff.

The Port Watch Tower of 1322 is now known as the Water Tower.

St Mary's Hill which led to the Shipgate is said to be England's steepest urban street.

During the 13th century Chester was famous for its fur trade and even by the mid-16th century the port was importing large amounts of fur and skins. In 1543 one ship alone brought in '1600 sheep fells, 68 dere, 69 fawne skins and 6300 broke (badger) fells'. Another, the following year imported '7 marten skins, 240 otters, 12 wolffe skins, 2 seales skins, 500 cony (rabbit) fells and 8 fox cases'. However by 1322 the river was silting up and moving away from the west wall so that John Helpstone was employed at a cost of £100 (perhaps £250,000 today) to build a port watch tower to protect the city.

1307 Murage duty taken on imported goods to upkeep walls.
c1310 Saint Werburgh's shrine built.
1311 Avowrymen (newcomers who had committed felonies elsewhere and fugitive bondmen from other villein-ages) given protection in Chester's palatinate.
1318 'Porte mote Court houlden first in this Cittye'. The court, under the mayor, judged breaches of the peace and registered land transactions. The Pentice Court dealt with debt, trespass and markets.
1321 Toll list for gates includes 'of every horselode of mussells one little dishefull ... of great fishe a quarter of a fishe or the headd or one penny.'

The state of the river did not improve and the 'ruinous state of the city and haven' was mentioned under Richard II in 1337. Already, trading ships were harbouring at Neston, Heswall, Croyton and regularly at Redcliff, 16 miles below Chester. The 'lamentable decay of the port by reason of the abundance of sand which has been allowed to choke up the creek' under Henry VI led to a decline in trade from 1400 onwards. Feefarm (tax) payments for the city were reduced, after petition, from £100 in 1300 to £50 in 1445, £30 in 1484 to a fixed £20 in 1486. Eventually, by 1569, downstream at Little Neston, 'New Haven' had been partially completed at the council's expense, taxes having been collected at 3½ᵈ per ton of imports and also from collections in churches during 1560.

The shipgate which stood beside the Old Dee Bridge probably dates to the early 13th century. It was demolished on 12th April 1831 and re-erected in Abbey Square gardens. It was then moved to the Grosvenor Park where it now stands.

The Chester Guilds also contributed towards the cost. But by 1604 the new port had still not been finished. In 1608, a year after the council opposed the creation of a port at Liverpool, the New Haven was becoming so dangerous that its partial demolition was ordered. In 1618 the Deputy Mayor of Liverpool wrote to Chester's Mayor reminding him that the harbours at Liverpool were an 'absolute and sole part of themselves and were never under the control of Chester.' By 1707 the New Haven was virtually redundant. Ships moved further downstream to Neston and later to Parkgate where packet boats ran to Ireland. Liverpool was growing.

Chester sailors had other problems. Her majesty's navy wanted recruits and it was easier if the men they 'conscripted' already knew how to sail. In 1703 a local merchant, Daniel Peck, wrote, 'I cannot engage one Ship here for London the Masters cannot gett men to go about land because the men are certainly prest the first place they touch att — If only a protection could be gott for a number of men to save the press I could meet with sevrall would come about — and if the charge was not too much I would have one for a Vessel of 150 ton.' Peck himself was, however, dependent on the services of the navy who, in 1704, supplied 'The Hector Man of War of 42 guns' to protect Chester convoys of merchantmen on their journeys to Plymouth and back.

The Water Tower at the canal entrance in the early 19th century.

In 1732 an Act of Parliament was passed to enable a new cut to be made to the river, reclaimed land being given to the 'Kinderly Undertakers' who were supposed to provide a standard depth of 16 feet. However, land reclamation for this 'River Dee Company' was a more profitable business and once a channel had been cut, they were more interested in land sales than navigation. A new Act was passed downgrading the depth to 15 feet but even this was never reached. The Admiralty alleged criminal negligence on the part of the River Dee Company who, in 1889, had their powers of management taken from them and given to a new Conservancy Board.

1322 Port Watch Tower (Water Tower) built for £100.
c1340 [Black Death kills a third of England's population.]
1352 Polychronicon written by monk Ranulph Higden.
1356 Pillory recorded at the cross.
1364 Ranulph Higden died.
c1375 Mystery Plays started.
1377 High Cross first mentioned.
1381 John Leche (king's surgeon) given annuity of £10 out of the Dee mills.
1384 Richard II allows the Black Friars to grind their corn free at the Dee mills.
c1390 Monks' seats 'misericords' carved with mythical scenes.
1399 Blue Bell built.

Square-rigged schooners, barquentines and sailing barges were still sailing to Crane Wharf quay in the 1880s, helped by the tugs Derby and Test from Saltney but by this time Liverpool was thriving and ocean going ships were larger. Any hope of Chester regaining its place as a maritime port had been lost.

Chester
Quay
C19th engraving

Note the boatbuilding on the Roodee in the distance.

Polychronicon

2am Matins then Lauds
6am Prime then Chapter Meeting
9am Terce
12am Sext
3pm None
6pm Vespers
7pm Compline

Within this tight schedule of services and devotion, the 14th century Benedictine monk, Ranulph Higden, wrote a seven volume history of the world, taking care to leave his name as an 'acrostic' inscribed at the initial letters of the first seven chapters: *Presentem Cronicam Coppilavit Frater Ranulphus Cestrensis Monachus.* Later, it was claimed (without any apparent evidence) that he had also written the mystery plays and travelled to Rome three times to seek permission to publish the plays in his native language, English. Higden spent 64 years as a monk and died around the Feast of St Gregory in 1363, having completed the Polychronicon (tales of many times) in 1340, although additions were made up to 1352. His tomb is in the present Chapel of St Erasmus at the cathedral. An English translation of the Polychronicon was printed in 1482. Two 15th century translations and the Latin version can be found in Chester Reference Library. A facsimile of the original is on display in the cathedral.

Opposite: Ranulph Higden at work in the 'scriptorium' of the abbey depicted in stained glass on a window in the cathedral slype.

Carved figure of Ranulph Higden on the outside wall of the cathedral south transept.

nine mens morris

Games played by adults in medieval and Tudor times included martial sports such as jousting, archery, wrestling, stone throwing, ball games and gambling for chance or easy skills, such as pitch and toss or shovelboard. 'Game' hunting was carried out throughout society with falconry and deer hunting for the nobles; the lower classes being used as keepers, beaters or dog handlers. Some of these pastimes are pictured in the Bayeux Tapestry. Bear and bull baiting is usually ascribed to the lower classes but at Westminster Hall in London during 1602 rebuilding included 'making a great place in the windowe for her Mat^ie against the bearebaitinge' whilst in Chester the Mayor watched the bull-baiting from the Pentice window. All classes engaged in cock-fighting.

Bearbaiting
From a 17th century woodcut.

A statute of Richard II prohibited serving men or labourers from playing tennis, football, quoits, dice and casting the stone. A later statute, of Henry VIII forbade apprentices playing 'tenys, clash, dice, cardes, bowles or such like unlawful games (except during the Christmas hollydayes and then only within their masters' houses). Also any householder allowing any of the above games in his house (except at Christmas) should be fined 6/8 for every offence.'

Chess, backgammon and merels were popular from courts to taverns and monasteries. Children played ball games, hoop rolling, tag, hide-and-seek and leapfrog as well as the usual noise, chase and scaring games.

Bullbaiting
From a 17th century woodcut.

While some games and sports were encouraged in the City of Chester, others were illegal. Every Maundy Monday after 1511 the sheriffs held a meat 'Breakfast' for the winners (who paid 2^d) and losers (paid 4^d) of an archery competition.

The Whitsun football match played until 1540 was becoming too 'inconvenient' for both the participants and the onlookers 'some haveinge their bodies bruised and crushed, some theire armes and legges broken' so Mayor Henry Gee replaced it with races on foot and on horseback.

Gamblers using cards, dice, bowls, 'le shoflebord' and 'super articulos' (on the knuckles, possibly jacks — although the records are often in English, some legal terms are still in Latin) ran the risk of being hauled in front of the sheriffs or the mayors to pay fines for 'carding, dysing and all such unlawfull games through out all the night wyth hauldinge and discoraging mens servants from their labour' although Lord Derby was allowed to keep bowling. (There was probably a difference between bowling and skittles — bowling in an alley.)

In 1561 Mistress Grymesdiche was fined for keeping a 'bowllying alleye unto the whiche Resorttes manye Craftismen Joureneye men And other younge men not mette neyther of abilities to use suche game as the bowlles' while Rico Haslewell was fined 13/4 as late as 1634.

Some gambling had been allowed in other cities so that, in 1616, the 'Virginian Companye' applied to run a 'Lottereye' in the Borough and offered to pay the city £40 for the privilege. There are no records to suggest that they succeeded, but a royal proclamation from 1620 in Chester Record Office, grants permission to hold a lottery to raise money for estates in Virginia.

1399 Bolingbroke (later Henry IV) takes Chester and brings back Richard II as prisoner on way to London. Head of Piers Legh, a supporter of Richard placed on castle tower.
1402 Writ for court of 24 jurors to be held at Dee (King's) Mills to ensure all grain was milled there.
1403 Welshmen to leave city on pain of decapitation.
1407 Defensive tower built on bridge.
1422 Mystery Plays performed on Corpus Christi Day.
1437 Wheat cost 7s a bushel so the poor made bread from peas, vetches (wild peas) and fern roots.
1449 North side of Pentice built.

When Bishop Norbury visited St Werburgh's Abbey at the beginning of the 14th century he found that the abbot had increasing debts and too many personal servants, and had also been eating meat in his own chambers during fish days. Among his new orders were no greyhounds or other dogs were to be kept by the abbot, monks or servants. The prior was to stay within the precincts and not, as in the past, go out hunting or make further use of bows and arrows.

So, in between services, meals and work, the monks would find a quiet corner to play games. Merels, also known as Nine Men's Morris or Nine Peg Morris, was one of these.

On a flat board three squares are drawn in increasing sizes from the same centre. A horizontal, a vertical and two diagonal lines cut the squares giving 24 stations where the lines cross. Each player, with nine pegs or markers, puts on pieces in turn to get three in a row, allowing him to take one of his opponent's pegs. Once all pegs are laid the players use their turn to move one peg to an adjacent station, without breaking an opposition line while pieces not forming a line remain. The game ends when the loser reaches two pegs. The game may have led to a Cheshire proverb 'Nichills in Nine Pokes' which is what eight million people get every week nowadays on the National Lottery.

Nine Men's Morris board carved in the cathedral.

eagle and child

A stained glass window in Stanley Palace supports a coat of arms with the legend of the eagle and child. It would seem that Sir Thomas Latham (1327-77), an ancestor to the Stanleys, only had a daughter, Isabell, with his wife. However his mistress, Mary Oscatell, had a son by him. In order to get his wife to adopt the child, the baby was put in an eagle's nest. When Sir Thomas and his wife 'found' the baby in the nest it was suggested that the eagle had stolen the babe. His wife had little option but to look after the poor orphan, who later became Sir Oscatell Latham.

The Tudor property with its long gallery was built in 1591. When Sir Peter Warburton of Gratton, Vice Chamberlain of Chester Exchequer and MP died in 1621, the property passed to his daughter and son-in-law, Sir Thomas Stanley of Alderly, a kinsman to the earl of Derby. Under threat of demolition and export to the USA it was purchased by the Chester Archaeological Society in 1866 and sold to the earl of Derby for £800 in 1889. In 1931 Edward, the 17th earl passed it to the City Corporation on a peppercorn rent for 999 years. Reconstruction took place in 1935. The English Speaking Union have leased the whole building since after World War II.

The Stanley Coat of Arms bear the motto of the Most Noble Order of the Garter.

Stanley Palace was known as Derby House in the 19th century.

Admiral of the Dee

The silver oar of Admiralty (1719) is an emblem of the Mayor's power over the estuary of the River Dee from Hoylake to Eccleston. Powers were said to have been granted by Edward, Prince of Wales, in 1342.

Richard Short, Lord Mayor and Admiral during 1997, takes to the water in a steam powered launch.

The silver oar, made by Richard Richardson around 1719, is 29cm long and inscribed with the city arms and names of the Water Bailiffs, Richard Stubs 1752 and James Meakin 1812. On the reverse of the oar are the arms of John Whitmore, mayor between 1369 and 1372 and his motto, 'Either for Ever.'

A charter by the Black Prince in 1353 confirms that '...Citizens, their heirs and successors that they may henceforward, as hitherto they have used without hindrance, make attachments in the Water of Dee between Chester and Arnoldseye for tolls and other customs belonging to the same citizens and duties on imports and also for offences committed in ships being in the said water...'

However a writer in the Cheshire Sheaf (1944) suggests that the term 'admiral' was merely quaint tradition and that this assumption was based on mention of persons appointed admirals and governors of the fleet in 1407 and that none of these were ever mayor. He may have been right, for the term 'admiral' means the commander of a fleet not just the owner of a port. In 1402 it was Thomas Capenhurst and John de Mollington who were appointed governors and chief admirals of a fleet supplied by the mayor and citizens of Chester, in 1407 Hugh de Multon, Thomas de Mukelfen, John Bran and John d'Acton were named as admirals and governors of the fleet.

Whether or not the term was ever used in documents, it is clear that the council had control over the river. In 1528 the Lord High Admiral confirmed that the 'liberties of the Mayor and citizens... were exempt from jurisdiction and power of the Admiral of England'. In 1638 the mayor refused to sign a writ to Sir Robert Grosvenor as 'Riparian owner of the water of Dee'.

The silver oar was carried by the Water Bailiff when exercising his power to arrest ships on the tidal Dee.

1474 [Caxton prints the first book in English.]
1482 Polychronicon printed.
1489 'This yeare St Peter's Steeple was pointed & by ye Parson & others a goose was eaten upon ye top thereof and part cast into ye 4 streetes'.
1498 Pentice rebuilt.
1499 The Midsummer Eve Watch, a colourful procession of freemen and guilds begun.
1500 [Black Lead pencils used in England.]
1503 Pavement laid from High Cross to Eastgate and St Michael's. Ex-mayors, ex-sheriffs and innkeepers to hang a lantern from dusk until 8pm, 1st November to 2nd February.

1506 Henry VII grants Great Charter to city, holding that the city be separate from the county, except the castle and Gloverstone. The citizens may elect a mayor, 24 aldermen, one a recorder, and 40 common councillors as well as 2 sheriffs, 2 coroners and 2 surveyors of the walls. The Recorder takes 1d toll for every ship in port, 1d for every merchant with goods and 1d for the ingate or outgate of every ton of wine, iron etc.
1508 'This yeare the first stonne of St Warbur's Steeple set and a bushell of wheat at 12d.' Lanterns to be hung out until 9pm.

'...they were divided into 24 pagiantes according to the companyes of the cittie ... every company had his pagiantor parte, which pagiants weare a high scafolde with 2 rowmes, a higher and a lower, upon 4 wheeles. In the lower they apparelled themselves and in the higher rowme they played, being all open on the tope, that all behoulders mighte heare and see them. The places where they played them was in every streete. They begane first at the abay gate: and when the first pagiante was played it was wheeled to the high crosse before the mayor and so to every streete'

mystery plays

THE MEDIEVAL CYCLE

Mystery Plays, or plays to translate the 'mysteries' of the Christian Holy Bible, were first performed in Italy as early as 1244. In 1264 a society 'Compagne del Gonfalone' was formed to act out Christ's sufferings during Passion week. It is not Known when plays were first performed in Chester or even whether the first ones were performed in Latin but this is doubtful as the audience, let alone the players, would not have understood them. Chaucer, in about 1390, says, 'Hast thou not heard (quod Nicholas) also The sorowe of Noe with his Fellowship Or that he might get his wife to ship' and makes other references to miracle or mystery plays. However, early stage directions for the Chester plays were written in Latin. Pre-reformation performances claimed that Henry Frauns or Francis, a monk of St Werburgh's Abbey during the late 14th century, had written the script. After the Reformation similar claims were made but now it was Ranulph Higden as the playwright and the mystery plays' first performance under the city's supposed first mayor, Sir John Arneway.

A record of 1422 shows that plays took place at the Feast of Corpus Christi and this appears to have continued until 1521. Plays on Corpus Christi Day in 1475 included 'The Trial and Flagellation of Christ' and 'The Crucifixion'. The plays were then expanded into a three day cycle on Whit Monday, Tuesday and Wednesday.

Each company or guild had to perform one play. Prior to the event the Crier read out the banns:

'The Aldermen and stewards of everie societie and Companie draw yourselves to your said severall Companies according to Ancient Custome and soe to appear with your said severall Companies everie man as you are Called upon paine that shall fall thereon.'

The early banns included an exhortation to each company to act their part well:

'The Waterleaders and Drawers of Dee loke that Noyes (Noah's) shipp be set on hie that you lett not the storye - and then shall you well cheve (achieve).'

In Noah's play, Noah and his sons load up all the provisions and the animals while his wife gossips with the neighbours. Noah urges her to hurry aboard:

**'The Flood comes in fleeting fast
On every side it spreadeth full fare
For fear of Drowning I am agast
Good gossip, let us draw near.'**

But Noah's wife carries on drinking and gossiping until, eventually, their sons carry her onto the ark by force.

1512 [According to Copernicus, the Earth goes round the Sun! Chocolate reaches Spain.]
1513 Henry Bradshaw, monk and poet, dies. He wrote 'The Life of Saint Werburgh' in verse.
1517 Grass grows a foot high at the Cross during the plague.
1521 'Life of St Werburgh' published.
1523 Roger Ledsham, abbey gatekeeper, drowns in pond.
1529 'Robert of Cicely' played at the High Cross.
c1530 Henry Dowes tutor of Gregory, son of Thomas Cromwell, in Chester reports that, 'I tell him ... history of the Romans ... he used to hawk and hunt, and shoot in his longbow... he seemeth to be thereunto given by nature'

Noah's play was traditionally performed by the Drawers of Dee (watercarriers). Fittingly the 'Three Kings' was played by the Mercers (tailors) and Spicers.

In 1564, a different type of pageant was put on: 27s 8d was paid for a spectacular on the Roodee devised by William Crafton and Mr More 'master of the art of history of Aeneas and Dido of Carthage'. In this waterborn fiery spectacle fourteen shillings worth of gunpowder was used when two forts were 'Raysed' and 'a ship on the water with sundry horsemen well apoynted.'

Noah's Ark in the 1997 Mystery Plays

Under Queen Elizabeth I the plays were seen as 'popery' and banned by the English Church. Despite this, a play cycle was performed in 1568, and the athedral paid for the stage and beer as in the previous performance of 1562. The plays were performed yet again, over four days, in 1575. This resulted in allegations against Mayor Savage who, as soon as his term as mayor expired, was called before the Privy Council in London. From there he wrote to the Chester Council to defend him, "*I am moste hartely to desyre you to sende me a certificate under your haundes and seale of your citie to testefy that the same Plays were sett forwarde as well by the Counsell ... I pray you may be sente me with as muche convenient spede as is possible*".

Luckily, he was supported by the Assembly, including the new protestant mayor, Henry Hardware, who certified that the plays had been authorised by the council.

Needless to say, this was the end of the Mystery Plays until their 20th century revival (except for a final showing of the Shepherd's Play before Lord Strange and his father, the earl of Derby, in 1577).

misericords

The medieval church is typified by the impressive quire at Chester Cathedral, formerly the Church of Saint Werburgh. It was here in the late 14th century that craftsmen set up intricately carved wooden stalls, each one with its own misericord or monk's mercy seat. Whilst appearing to stand for services, the monks could rest on the ledges of the upturned seats. The
woodcarvers had been at Lincoln and went on, after three years, to Westminster Hall. Forty-three original scenes remain on the underside of the seats, and there are five modern replacements. As well as religious themes there is a rich tapestry of legend, many from pre-Christian times : grotesque figures, hunting scenes, knights and kings, a lady chastening her spouse; as well as creatures real and mythical — lions and dogs, griffins, wyverns and winged beasts.

Is it an elephant or Sir Yvain caught in a portcullis? Is the foxy hooded figure a sly friar catching out the unwary whilst preaching to them, or Pandora's box in the hands of the fox-faced Epimetheus? Does the grotesque sticking out his tongue (similar to the roof bosses at St John's Church, see front cover) represent a gorgon figure as in the Roman temple at Bath (and derive from the Hindu goddess of death, Kali)? Many of these scenes are repeated at Nantwich, Carlisle, Exeter, Bristol, Worcester, Lincoln and Lancaster but there is still disagreement about their meaning.

However, like the borders of the earlier Bayeux Tapestry, it is likely that the artists drew on a wide range of literature and myth, providing us with some insight into the tales, legends and folklore of the medieval period.

The carving of Saint Werburgh (see page 17) is unique to Chester.

Each scene on the misericords is supported by two smaller scenes such as the oak-leaved head (top) and the wyvern, split to show both sides (below).

Stuck in a portcullis

On the bench ends are more carvings, including an elephant and castle (this one is the castle or carriage carried on the elephant's back – the carver, however, never having seen an elephant used a horse's body as a base). There is a pelican restoring life to its chick with blood from its own breast: a symbol of Christian piety. A magnificent Jesse tree on the Abbot's stall shows Christ's family tree growing from the loins of Jesse, through King David and his ancestors to the Virgin Mary, thus fulfilling biblical prophecy.

One carved scene shows the legend of the unicorn. The mythical beast has an allegorical meaning as it represents Christ brought to Earth by a virgin and sacrificed by man: 'The horn of the unicorn is so powerful that the hunters dare not go near it but the animal can be caught. A pure virgin of great beauty is sent to the centre of the wood where the Unicorn dwells and as soon as it sees her it runs towards her and kneels down and lays its head on her lap. While the Unicorn sleeps there the hunters seize her.'

Imp

High in the Romanesque triforium of the Cathedral, amid the arches at first floor level, in the northern wall, is a 'curious carving which represents a man, all huddled together bound hand and foot'.

At one time this figure would have overlooked the quire which was in the easternmost bay of the nave. Apparently 'the devil was always consumed with a desire to witness the celebration of the eucharist. He could not watch it through the choir windows, each of which was guarded by an angel. But the nave windows were unguarded. Coming from the north (the devil's quarter) he would walk straight for the easternmost window of the nave, in the hope that by screwing his head close against the glass he might see into the choir, over the choir screen. Imagine him peering in; he starts back suddenly; the first object to meet his gaze is this figure huddled up, bound head and foot. He flies off in terror, recognising the penalty that awaits him if he should profane the mysteries with his gaze.'

1533 Corn to be sold only in the market and sales not to start until the bell is rung. Private citizens have first choice, then bakers, then others.

1534 A fish market, the King's Fish'board, recorded.

1536 [Authority of the Pope banned by Parliament.]

1540 Rauf Wryne, the Recorder, officiates as clerk to the sheriffs in the Pentice Court. Children over six must work or attend school 'to learne ther belefe & other devocions prayers and learnings or els to such other good and vertuus laborure craft or occupacyon'. Murengers toll: 'everye but sanmond viiijᵈ' (8ᵈ per salmon boat).

In Lincoln Cathedral there is also an imp, said to be the devil turned to stone on seeing the mysteries.

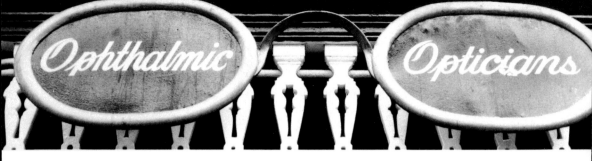

Spectacles

Sign above Siddall Opticians, in Bridge Street since 1815.

A long-sighted Black Friar from Chester may have worn glasses with convex lenses in the mid-15th century. A fragment of bone spectacles were found in the remains of the Dominican Friary. They would have come from a pair carved in bone and riveted to sit astride the nose. This is one of the earliest fragments found from a dated site and probably came from the Netherlands where glasses were exported as early as 1400.

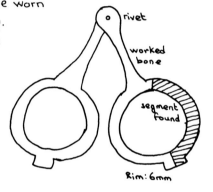

Sketch of the medieval spectacles.

A pair of biconvex glasses were found in the excavation of the former market hall. They may date to the mid-17th century.

Turn of the 19th century spectacles, hallmarked with a lion passant, in the window display at Worden Optometrists in St Werburgh Street.

The Blue Bell

As the Chester historian, Thomas Hughes, wrote: 'The Anglo-Saxons had their eala-hus (ale house), win-hus (wine house) and cumen-hus (inn) but there are no records of their whereabouts.' According to the Domesday Book, before 1066 any maker of bad beer was put in the cucking stool or fined four shillings. By 1379, in Chester, a gallon of white wine cost 6^d and claret 4^d.

Chester's sole remaining medieval inn was originally called the Bell, a common name for inns near churches, and one of over 500 names recorded for the city pubs over the years. Names such as the Sun, Moon and Angel have gone along with the Horse & Bags, Dairy Maid, Brewer's Dray, Corkcutters' Arms and Blackamore's Head which reflect on their time period.

The Bell may well have been supplied from the abbey opposite who had a brewhouse near the medieval 'Little' gateway still remaining. The inn building has a braced kingpost from the late 14th or early 15th century but parts of the building may date from the 11th century. The date 1494 refers to the first type of pub licensing created by an Act of Parliament. Justices of the Peace were able to 'put away common ale selling where they should think convenient?'

The Blue Bell,
now a restaurant,
in Northgate Street.

The City Assembly tried to stop beer houses being used for other purposes with the byelaw: 'wher as all the tavernes and ale housis of this citie have and be used to be kept by young women, otherwise then is used by eny other place in this relme, wherof all strangers resorting hether greatly marvil and think it an unconvenyent use, whereby not onely grete slander and dishonest report of this citie hath and doth run a brode ... it is ordered ... that no tavarns nor ale-howses be kept ... by eny women being betwene fourteen and forty yeres of age?

Another Assembly order, in 1569, banned members or officials from frequenting any ale or beer house, and in 1575 innkeepers were reminded that no shop or tavern was to be kept open during divine services or sermon. In 1590 the Assembly reached out to the common man and ordered that 'ale to be no more than a penny a quart and it to be full?

William Bird of 'Ye Bell Innholder' was admitted to the Innkeepers Guild in 1596. However when, at another pub in 1614, William Johnson petitioned that he had served an apprenticeship for George Brooke, an innholder, and asked admission as a freeman of the city, the council refused. It was considered that the innkeeping trade was not a fitting one for an apprentice as it was neither art, mystery nor occupation by which it was possible to advance the common wealth of the city. How then, anyone could become a new innkeeper at that time is not clear but the Brewers' Guild was incorporated in 1635 and in 1692 it was confirmed that only freemen were licensed to sell beer.

Outside the Blue Bell, Elizabeth Haliwell built a barber's shop in the stall before her dwelling house in 1680/1. Later, it is said, the small cabin was used to sell coaching tickets, the small upper window to reach passengers travelling with the baggage on the coach roof.

It would seem that there were still some who preferred to miss out on a church sermon, for, in 1759, the constables of the city were to 'make diligent search upon every Sunday in the time of Divine Service in the severall streets ... and in all tiplinghouses ... and ... apprehend such loose, idle or disorderley persons' that they found.

GIANTS

great hoopes dale bords Couper worke
nayles
size cloth
bastbord paper for bodyes
sleve and skirts to be Cuellered Tinsilld Arsedine Cullers
Arsenik to put into the paste to save the giants from being eaten
by Ratts

The monk, Lucian, told of a procession of clerics from St John's Church to St Mary-on-the-hill in 1195, and annals mention a parade in 1397/8, but it was not until 1499* that the 'Wach on Midsummer Eve was first sett out & begonne'. This was a procession organised by the city guilds and took place in the years when the Mystery Plays were not shown, and continued after their demise. A cultural feature of the city, these colourful noisy parades linked the church, the civil authority and the people. With a lead drum and a flag ('the Aunciente'), soldiers and animals, this was the highlight of the year.

On the 21st April 1564 the giants needed repair, having been well used. Thomas Poole and Robert Hallwood agreed to provide '4 gyants, 1 unikorne, 1 dramodarye, 1 Luce, 1 camell, 1 dragon, 6 hobby horses and 16 naked boys' and carry them from place to place that year and in the future. For this they were paid 40 shillings (each year). City and guild records hold long lists of payments made to organise the procession but, in 1601, the Morris dancers, who previously were paid a small sum, had 'no fee but the curtesye after the show...'

1541 St Werburgh's Monastery, surrendered in 1540, becomes Cathedral of Christ and the Blessed Virgin Mary. King's School starts.
1545 New Common Hall in St Nicholas' Chapel.
1552 The plague in the city called Stubbes' byle.
1555 Protestant preacher, George Marsh, tried, convicted and burnt for heresy at Boughton.
1556 Country bakers invited to attend market.
1558 Port of Chester brought into national customs' system.
1564 'A great frost this yeare and dee frozen so that they played at football thereon.'

*It began under the mayorality of Richard Goodman who served from November 1498 until November 1499.

Putting together the show was profitable for some and fun for others. An account by Randle Holme includes:

'Buckram for the Giants hoods — 4 0

Fine buckram for the Giants whiskers at 2d in thrid — 10 10

4 Dale boards to make stayes to carry the giants with and double and single spiks and stone nayles — 4 8

Michael Linch for cutting the garnish whiskers and all the roses used about the work — 10 0

George Malbone, 35 days at 6d per diem — 17 6

John Banion, 15 dayes worke at 1/- — 15 00

John Wright, 35 days chiding and brawling and hindering the workmen from their work, and allsoe for fuddleing and drinkinge with several other leters and molestationers, just nothing and worthily he declareth it — 00 00

But the fun was not appreciated by all and the protestant Mayor Henry Hardware banned the parade in 1600. However, the next mayor, Robert Brerewood, revived the tradition but forbade the devil in feathers and the naked boys. The watch was again banned under Cromwell after the Civil War but reinstated again under Charles II. The last of these Midsummer shows was recorded in 1670, they were then moved to Whit Tuesday until 1678. They were not revived until 1995.

1564 A new 'great bord' 'set in the fyshe market' for 3ˢ8ᵈ.

1567 Four taverns licensed in Chester.

1568 Northgate Street and White Friars paved.

1569 Every member of the Assembly to provide and maintain fire buckets. The two sheriffs fight and are fined £10 towards repairing the walls. City Treasurer's accounts: 'For making the north-gate bridge new, grette joists thick planks iiiiˡ iiiˢ ijᵈ' (£4/3/2).

1572 Sᵗ John's tower collapses.

1573 Pentice enlarged.

1576 William Golborne and David Dymock, the two city sheriffs, imprisoned for refusing to levy fines.

There was also a Christmas Eve Watch: a candlelit procession would go from the mayor's house to the Common Hall where the keys to the city gates would be given to the mayor who, in turn, entrusted them to the watchmen who would keep the city safe over yuletide. The parade then returned to the mayor's house.

The Midsummer Watch participants gather on
the filled-in abbey pond. The city has a family
of giants: a father, a mother and two daughters.
In the background is the Cathedral (the former
abbey) and the column which is said to have
come from the Exchange (a forerunner to the
Town Hall).

1503 'evry man that hath byne mayre or shriffes of the citie of Chester and allso all innkeepers as well they that have sygnez as they that have no sygnez shall have hanging at ther dore a lantorne wyth a candyll bryning in it every nyghte from that it be furst nyght unto the oure of 8 of the clocke, that is to wyt from the feste of All Sayntes unto the fest of the Puryfycaccion of Our Lady then nexte folying yerlye'.

[Nov 1 - Feb 2]

1537 'Ordered, That all Public Houses shall hang out their lantornes and Candles from six of the clocke in the evening until nine of the clocke every night betwen the feast of All Saints and the Purification of the Virgin Mary.'

1540 'a lantorne wyth a candyll byrning in it every nyghte until 8 o'clock'

1617 Adam Caine the Beadle was paid 2s6d for 'providing of candles to the city's lantern at the new stairs.'

1704 Two convex lamps to be provided and set up at the city's charge – one at the corner of the new Pentice and the other at the Exchange. Regulations that councillors and publicans should hang lanterns were cancelled on a 25-24 vote.

1724 'payd for mending the Lantharn in the pentice 0:1:6'

1737 Nathaniel Hall leased a messuage with appurtenances on the north side of Eastgate Street and had to 'set up before the front of the said messuage a Lamp with convex Glasses of the same sort and size as is now

Bridge Street Fountain and Gaslight of 1854, demolished for road widening.

used in the City of London and supply the
same with oil and keep the same burning
from three large weeks [wicks] of Cotton...
to the hour of ten between the tenth
day of September and the tenth day
of March?

1762 Act 'And it is hereby further enacted
    by the Authority aforesaid, That if any
    Person or Persons shall wantonly,
    wilfully, carelesly, or maliciously,
    break, throw down, extinguish, damage,
    displace or spoil any lamp that shall
    be hung out, fired or set up to light
    the Streets, Rows or Passages, in
    the said City... forfeit the sum of
    five pounds?

Lamp at The Boot.

[1801 London had its first gas street lighting.]
1853 Assembly minutes 'that the recomendation of the Watch Committee to accept
Mr Highfield's offer to light the City for two years with not less than two hundred
and eighty three and not more than Two hundred
and ninety three Batwing Burners at a cost not
exceeding £786 per annum being the expense of
lighting the City last year be accepted'

1854 An order was made
to change some of the
Batwings to Fishtails.

1896 Forty-eight electric
arc lights used as
street lights.

Lamp at the Oddfellows Arms.

Carved electric
lamp, Newgate St.

Gargoyles

Medieval gargoyles*are drainage spouts representing humans or animals, often mythic, with their mouths open to let out the water. False gargoyles are purely for decoration. Corbels support a beam.

Look around the city, especially on the inside or outside of the cathedral, the churches, shops and inn fronts to see a wealth of stone and wood carvings — too many to fit in this book.

Photos by Simon Atkinson.
Opposite from left to right, top to bottom:

Carved bench end, Cathedral quire, said to represent a C14th musician and his choirmaster who regularly argued.
Gargoyle, Cathedral.
Three corbels/heads from St Michael's Church, Bridge St.
Modern cast head from the Prudential office in Crook St.
The head of Christ or St Benedict perhaps, from the medieval abbey gateway.
Modern cast head from T.J. Hughes, Hamilton Place.
Wyvern from St Michael's Church, Bridge Street.
A king (or king of the woods) from the Cathedral
Lion, probably representing Mark the evangelist under the fixed sign of Leo, in the Cathedral nave.

* Compare the enormous amount of onomatopoeic words — gargle gurgle, jugular, jug, goglet, goblet, gobble, gag, gutter, gutteral, gob and juggler — all from the sound of a throat.

1577 390 beer houses in Cheshire.
1578 Whole Company of Butchers interred in Northgate Gaol for not supplying a sufficient quantity of meat for the citizens.
1579 Watergate Street paved from the Cross to Trinity Church.
1580 [Francis Drake completes world tour.] Arms granted to city with motto 'Antiqui Colant Antiquum Dierum' (Let the ancients honour the ancient of days).
1581 East end of St John's cut off from the church which is bought from Queen Elizabeth to create parish church.
1582 Water conduit from Boughton brought to next to St Peter's.

1584 Eastgate Street 'new paved' and the central gutter laid. Robert Dudley, Earl of Leicester and favourite of the queen, visits Chester and banquets with mayor. A storm of 5 inch (12.5cm) hailstones. Abbey pond filled in.
1585 A clock erected on St Peter's.
1587 A hundred soldiers maintained for the defence of the city to receive 6d a day for training. A man was hanged, drawn and quartered for clipping money and his quarters were set on 4 gates.
1589 Queen's Players visit city with feats of tumbling and ropedancing.
1590 [First English paper mill in Kent.]

83

before the Reformation

Although Braun's map of 1581 is not entirely accurate and was drawn 40 years after the Reformation, it shows Chester's main buildings. Much of the land space used by the pre-Reformation religious houses can be seen.

There were five parish churches which may have been around in Saxon times: St Werburgh's (with St Oswald's within), St Peter's, St Olaf's (named after King Olaf of Sweden, died 1070, making the dedication after the Conquest), St Bridget's (now demolished, named after an Irish saint), and St John (formerly the minster, later Chester's first cathedral). There were also the parish churches of St Mary-on-the-hill (which started life inside the castle where traces of wall paintings in the chapel can still be seen), St Michael's (recently the Heritage Centre), St Martin's (now demolished) and Holy Trinity (now the Guildhall).

In the northeast of the city the Benedictine Abbey of St Werburgh (now the Cathedral Church of Christ and the Blessed Virgin Mary) took up nearly a quarter of the old Roman fortress site, while in the southwest, the Benedictine Nunnery of St Mary stood above the Roodee. Over four centuries the abbey had become rich. Compare the 1535 income of St Werburgh's Abbey at £1073. 17s. 7½d with St Mary's Nunnery whose income for the same year stood at under £100.

There were also three hospices run by monks or nuns: St Giles (a leper hospital out at Boughton), St Ursula's and Little St John's (where the Bluecoat Hospital is today).

The Black Friars were situated on the south side of Watergate Street. In 1384 Richard II had given them a charter, 'that they shall have leave to grind all the corn and grain they need for their sustenance at our Mills in Chester, free from all toll and customs...' North of Watergate Street were the Grey Friars (not in today's street of the same name). They had arrived in the city by 1238 and in 1245 Henry II let them take stone from the castle ditch to build their houses and chapel. The friars allowed fishermen to keep their nets

ARMA EPISCOPATVS

Braun's Map of 1581

Hogenberg had a hand in it too

and tackle in the buildings on condition that the fishermen kept these buildings in good repair. By 1538 they had a quire, a vestry, a kitchen, brewhouse, buttery and poultry house. The White Friars, with their undyed cassocks or robes, founded their Chester friary just off Bridge Street in 1277, perhaps with the best pickings for their begging and preaching rounds.

Many deals had been struck in 1538. The Dissolution was imminent. The buildings, gardens and orchards of the three friaries were sold to a John Cokkes of London for £356.6s.10d, but it was local gentry who managed to rent estates from St Werburgh's Abbey for long periods in exchange for small sums. By law, any leases made a year before the surrender of the abbey would stand after the Dissolution. Perhaps then, it comes as no surprise that the 'visitor' to the abbey, Dr Legh, who had himself signed a 99 year lease for two manors, managed to postpone the abbey closure for 14 months.

The Cathedral was founded a year later. Ten monks were kept on for new duties in the Cathedral including the abbot who became the dean. Eleven monks were pensioned off and seven others may have become priests or curates.

The former nunnery and friaries became private homes for the rich or had their lead roofs melted and stone reused. The Parish Church of St Mary-on-the-hill managed to buy the whole quire roof from Basingwerk Abbey in North Wales which was closed in 1536. The carved letter bosses on the roof now spell MARIA. The 'curiously wrought ornamental spire' of White Friars served as a useful point of reference for sailors on the Dee and was only finally demolished in 1597, after Braun's map was drawn.

Medieval Chester had nine parishes but new boundaries were fixed by order of the Privy Council in 1882. St Peter's was the only parish entirely within the city walls. Parish boundary markers, such as this one for St Michael's Parish in Bunce Street, can be found on the walls of houses in the city. There is one on the 'Nine Houses' in Park Street. Nowadays Chester is all one team parish.

Pied Bull

The oldest licensed house in Chester still serving beer has an even older history. Richard the Butler granted lands to the Nuns of St Mary's in c1155 on his mother Gunnora taking the veil. There were two dwellings, divided into three. In 1267 Roger the Barber was granted a house on the site of 'le Lorimersrowe'. By 1533 it was known as Bull Mansion, the house of the city recorder (see page 133). Richard Grimsditch is the first publican mentioned in the Innkeepers Accounts of 1571. The nearby Beast Market led to a plethora of pub names in the vicinity: the White Bull a few doors away, the Bull's Head down the street, the Bull & Stirrup outside the Northgate and the Brown Cow opposite that, as well as the Bull & Dog (now the Liverpool Arms). Constantine Huygens, secretary to King William, stayed at

Mr Lloyd's house in Abbey Square during 1690 but he ate at the Pied Bull. By 1784 John Paul was running a four horse coach to Birkenhead from the Pied Bull. A plaque outside the building gives another claim to fame: George Borrow may have stayed here before his tour of 'Wild Wales' in 1854.

Beneath the Tudor staircase, some say they can feel a chill presence as they enter the cellar. The Coroners' report of 1609 found that John Davies 'casually fell down a pair of stairs leading to the Sellar belonging to the Pide Bull Inn and with a knife in his hand ...and dyed.' But perhaps it is just the cold draught from the open cellar grating.

The Tudor staircase above the cellar door.

Belman & Crier

In 1540 fees due to the bellman included:
of every worshipfull gentyllman that goyth onye
gounes at ther buryall   … one goune
[at funerals gowns would be given to mourners]
of every worshipfull gentyllman that gevth no
gones then he to have for going with the bell …iiijd (
of every pore man that he goyth for with his bell …jd (
when he goythe for aneything that is lost …jd
for every bote lode with powder mellwylle
        (salted fish)   … one fyshe
for every boute lode with fresh fyshe that he
        goeth for   …jd

In 1556 a record shows 'To ye belman for p'claimyng ye Fownder's dyryge 27 Januarrij …i
(on Henry VIII's death, the founder of King's School).

On 7th October 1681 John Whitehead was confirmed as the city's Day Bellman. An order by the Assembly – that for ornament and securing the city from fire all new houses in the main streets were to be tiled, not thatched, and that all existing houses should be reroofed – was to 'be published throughout the city by the bellman' to ensure that all were aware of the new byelaw. John was granted a new coat and badge as his predecessor wore. George Tunnall took over the post in 1685. In 1697 one public notice given by Tunnall forbade tipping rubbish between the bridge and the Roodee. In 1700 he was required to post an order against breaking up or making holes in the pavements for erecting stalls at the fairs upon pain of 6s8d. From 1704 Tunnall paid 12d a week to the retired John Whitehead but this sum was soon mitigated to 6d, then nothing at all, and Mr Whitehead became an almsman. In the same year it was ordered that no cattle were to be 'ley'd' on the Roodee except for the full ley. Notice was posted and Tunnall was to publish it every Saturday until the next May Day. Tunnall continued as bellman until his death in 1708. Thomas Booth took the office until he died in 1715 then John Fearnall Jnr, who was granted a coat annually instead of tri-annually as previously. £1:4:0 was paid for three yards of 'cloath' and a further six shilling for making it into a coat. James Bateman took over from 1721 until 1734. In 1722 a shilling was paid for 'Boyling the Bellman's Badge.'

In the late 16th or early 17th century Robert Lowe the 'night belman' gave a written undertaking to return the 'silver badge with the citties arm or thereupon engraven' if he lost his job. Mr Sutton was confirmed as the Night Bellman in 1655, but he must have been doing the job for some time because a year later his widow claimed the outstanding part of his three years' pay at 26s 8d annually – apparently he had only received 6s 8d. Ralph Joynson held the post from 1663. The year 1711 saw the death of John Beagh, the Night Bellman for 20 years. William Wiswall was confirmed in the office and was paid £1:6:0 in four quarterly payments. Other fees were collected elsewhere and the treasury paid him 2s 6d for 'proclaiming St George's Fare at ffarndon'. Prescott, a Chester diarist records that, on 18th November 1715, the 'Belman at the Cross near us Reads publicly a proclamation in the Mayor's name, commanding all persons in the City to bee of peacable and civil behaviour, not to walk about the Streets or Rows at unreasonable Hours of the night'. Thomas Posnitt took over the bellman's position. Perhaps the bellman did not have as much work, because he became the day bellman as well in 1734. He carried on for nine years until his death. John Posnitt then took over as 'Day and Night Bellman'.

Meanwhile there was also the Crier: the Smiths, Cutlers and Plumbers paid the crier 13d for 'ridunge the banes' (reading the banns of the Mystery Plays) in 1553. Richard Woodcock, in 1598, had 'a tymber mast typt at both endes and embellished in the middest with silver wherof Thomas Richardson late Cryer had the use and custody to be kepte and used by the said Richard Woodcock as the Cities goods and to be delivered back to the same citie upon demand'. The 1606-7 accounts of the 'Drawers of Dee' state 'geven to the Crier ijd'. At the cross bullbait in 1620 a fight started between the butchers and the bakers, and the 'Cryer brake his Mace in peeces Amonge them'. The butchers later supplied another bull to bait.

The London Bellman in 1603

By the King.

A Proclamation againſt Steelets, Pocket Daggers,
Pocket Dagges and Piſtols.

He loue and care Wee haue towards the preſerua-tion of Our Subiects, and the keeping of Our Lande from being polluted with blood; doth make Us ſtriue with the euill humors and depraued cuſtomes of the times, to reforme and ſuppreſſe them by Our Princely policy and Juſtice; To which end and purpoſe, we haue by the ſeueritie of Our Edict, (proceeding from Our owne pen, and by the exemplar cenſure and Decrees of Our Court of Starre-Chamber) put downe, and in good part maſtered that audacious cuſtome of Duelles and Challenges, and haue likewiſe by a Statute made in Our time, taken away the benefit of Clergie in caſe of Stabbing, and the like odious Man-ſlaughters:

Wherefore it being alwayes the more principall in Our intention to preuent, then to puniſh, being giuen to vnderſtand of the vſe of Steelets, pocket Daggers, and pocket Dags and Piſtols, which are weapons vtterly vnſeruiceable for defence, Militarie practiſe, or other lawfull vſe, but odious, and noted Inſtruments of murther, and miſchiefe; we doe ſtraightly will and command all perſons whatſoeuer, that they doe not henceforth preſume to weare or carie about them any ſuch Steelet or pocket Dagger, pocket Dagge or Piſtoll, vpon paine of Our Princely Indignation and diſpleaſure, Impriſonment and Cenſure in the Starre-Chamber; And we doe likewiſe ſtraightly forbid vpon like paine all Cutlers, or other perſon, to make or ſell any of the ſaid Steelets, pocket Daggers, pocket Dagges or Piſtols.

Giuen at Our Pallace of Weſtminſter, the 26. day of March, in the fourteenth yeere of Our Reigne of Great Britaine, France and Ireland.

God ſaue the King

Imprinted at London by ROBERT BARKER, Printer to the Kings moſt Excellent Maieſtie. ANNO DOM. 1616.

A proclamation of 1616/17   Chester Record Office MP1

A List of fees for 1621 shows that the Portmote Court paid 12^d 'to the crier' while the Crownmote Court paid 4^d. In 1632, after Thomas Knowesly died, Ralph Minshull took over, receiving 10^s a year, until at least 1646. Robert Moulson took payment for the position in 1662 and was confirmed as City Crier in 1665.

In 1690, Robert Warmingham, Crier, petitioned the Assembly to ensure that he received his proper dues which, owing to the removal of the fruit market to Northgate Street, people were refusing to pay. It was ordered that all foreigners coming to the market should pay the crier his usual toll and that the Treasurers should pay him 20^s four times a year. The following year he was granted a toll of a shilling on all ton loads of coal entering the city, with 9^d, 8^d or 6^d on smaller loads.

In 1702 William Willoughby took over as Common Crier from William Warmingham who had taken office in 1699. The year 1713-14 saw Willoughby petition the Assembly. He had looked after the city fire engine for seven years without payment and even paid to have it housed one year. The Assembly granted his expenses and a yearly salary of ten shillings.

In 1792 John Yarwood became Day and Night Bellman, William Ratcliffe the Crier. John Cartwright was appointed Bellman in 1818. George Topham resigned as Crier in 1825 but was reappointed the same month. A report of 1835 showed that the Crier was appointed at Assembly and paid 15^s annually.

The Crier and Bellman must have always done similar work and the two positions may now have been the same. Records in the 19th century are vague although in 1859 an annual fee of £1 6^s 0^d and endowments from the office of bellman was paid while the Corporate Estate Committee papers give the bellmen for 1863-97. A photograph from about this time, now on the City Record Office Image Bank, shows 'The Last Bellman' complete with a full white beard, wearing a top hat and coat and carrying a proclamation and his bell.

Go to the Town Crier Public House opposite the station to see the 1990 Crier in his blue uniform. In May 1997, while keeping David Maguire the Crier, the council, based on the research in this book, appointed David Mitchell as the first bellman for a century.

Chester's first Bellman for a century, David
Mitchell (on the left, holding the proclamation)
is now the Town Crier and Bellman while
David Maguire (on the right, holding the bell)
was the Town Crier until early 1998.

In 1999 David Mitchell came third at the World Town Crier
Championship in Canada. His wife Julie, who also makes their
uniforms, came sixth. They are the world's only married criers.

Chester Races

Henry Gee, Mayor of Chester in 1540 cancelled the traditional Shrove Tuesday game, where 'one ball of lether caulyd a fout boule to play from thens [the Roodee] to the Comen hall' because it was becoming increasingly violent. He replaced it with 'a bell of sylver to the value of 3s 4d ... to whom shall run best and furthest upon horsebak'.

In 1607 a 'new gallerie was built on the Roodee at the city's expense'.   In 1609 an additional race was run with 'Saincte Georges bells and vase of running horses with other pleasant shows invented by Mr Robert Amerye iremonger and sometime sheriff, all these at his coste'.

The sheriffs gave a plate valued at £13 6s 8d in 1640 for an Easter Tuesday race to replace the traditional 'sheriffs breakfast' archery competition. In 1714 the Corporation Plate was added, with 24 guilds donating £25 annually. A register of racing colours existed in 1762. Entrance fees for runners during 1777 were 2 guineas for subscribers and 3 guineas for non-subscribers.

Even then, parking charges were in force: John Edmon, Keeper of the Roodee was at liberty to collect 'one day at each Races one Shilling for every Carriage going on the Roodee. And that in Consideration thereof he do not only the Duty of a Keeper of the Roodee but also the Labourers Work which shall be necessary.'

Autumn 1780 saw the Gold Cup introduced; this was later run in the spring. The year 1802 saw the Earl of Chester's Plate run for 100 guineas.

In 1822 George Brooke, on behalf of 'the Country Gentlemen who attend Chester Races

Racegoers in Northgate Street, Cup Day 1846

and those that send their horses' petitioned to have 'Races before dinner after half past two so that the half day's work could be done and those attending the Races have the morning to walk around town to make purchases from the shops. Country persons might then dine in town? Needless to say, this petition favouring employers and traders was quickly granted.

This Bewick woodcut shows horses galloping with all legs out-stretched. Muybridge's photos of a galloping horse in 1872 showed that this never happens. (See Chester Inside Out)

The first paying gate meeting was for the newly-formed Chester Race Company Ltd in the spring of 1893. Despite the one shilling minimum charge, crowds of about fifty thousand turned up over three days but thousands still managed to get in for nothing. Even the Chief Constable admitted to opening the gates and letting in about 200 racegoers for free to stop a woman being crushed at the turnstile.

On course betting

The following year a new tradition was started. The Tradesmen's Cup, which had begun in 1824, had, under the new company become the Chester Cup: a large silver punch bowl weighing over nine kilos was the prize. Now further prizes of large Cheshire Cheeses were given to winner and places.

Disaster struck when the County Stand, built in 1899 for £12,500, burnt down in 1985. The new stand cost millions and was built in excellent taste to reflect on the character of Britain's oldest racecourse.

The modern County Stand.

BLUE POSTS

In 1558, Dr Henry Coles, Dean of St Paul's Cathedral, was charged with a commission by Queen Mary to the Council of Ireland to prosecute Irish protestants. While he was staying at the Blue Posts Inn he was overheard by Mrs Mottershead, the proprietor, to say, "Here is what will lash the heretics of Ireland". Fearing for her brother in Dublin, Mrs M stealthily removed the commission and replaced it with a pack of cards, a black jack uppermost. When the Dean reached the Lord Deputy in Ireland he found he had been tricked and returned to get proof of his commission. However, by that time, the protestant Queen Elizabeth I was on the throne. Mrs Mottershead was awarded a life pension from the grateful new queen.

Left: Mrs Mottershead.

A 19th century artist shows the Blue Posts Inn in Lower Bridge Street but historians claim it was in the upper part of Bridge Street beside Feathers Lane. Engraving courtesy of David Cummings.

Leche House

HAND & SNAKE

The underlying structure of Leche House, with its five bay undercroft, dates from the 14th century. John Leche (Leech) was the surgeon to Edward III and was, in 1381, granted £10 a year from the Dee Mills. George Leche's will of 1551 bequeathed rents and over 24 houses in Chester including the house 'of *Ric Brynes ye younger in Watergate Street.*' Most of the four-storey timber building may have been rebuilt for Sir John Leche in the 1570's. Inside was a hidden priest hole, used to hide Roman Catholic priests in the 17th and 18th centuries. The grille on the far wall is a squint or spy hole which uses the bars like a one-way mirror. It was used as a watch place when 'illegal' Catholic services were held.

1590 'Ale to be no more than a penny a quart and it to be full'. 'Harry Bonoventure', a privateer from Chester, is manned with 60 crew, 12 guns and 6 months' supplies to be used 'in warlike manner agaynste the Kinge of Spayne'.

1591 Stanley Palace built. A hook with rings for pulling down buildings is added to the city's fire equipment.

1592 'In this yeare the new buildings neere the milke stoopes in Eastgate streete new builded at the Cittyes Charge'.

1595 Plays and bearbaiting prohibited.

The Squint

The impressive painted chimney front in the galleried hall has the motto 'Alla corona Fidessimo' (most faithful to the crown) with a vine and grapes, roses and leaves, and a gorgon's head as well as a painted hand and snake. In 1723 the Hand & Snake public house was in the building.

The Fireplace.   Photos taken courtesy of Sofa Workshop.

Wolfgate

The old gate of the city, near the amphitheatre, goes by three names.

Does the name Wolfgate come from a wolf carving, said to be the arms of Hugh Lupus, first Norman earl of Chester, and taken down when the gate was rebuilt? Others claim that it is named after Wolfius (Wolfsy), Bishop of Chester from 1039 to 1053, or even from a Scandinavian name 'Ulfaldi'? It could also come from wool field gate. In 1303 Mabel Harald payed 6^d for a garden in 'Wolfuldegate'.

The gate was also known as the Newgate. In 1552 'iiij (4) bordes for making the Newgatt' cost 13^{s}8^d. Rebuilding of the complete structure was allowed on the 24th January 1608/9.

The Wolfgate.

This gate, at the end of Pepper Street, was also called the Peppergate. It gained notoriety when, in 1573, Ellen, the daughter of Mayor Aldersey eloped through it with her lover, leaving the Assembly to order, on the 15th January 1573 that the gate be shut! This gave rise to a Chester proverb about shutting the Peppergate after the daughter had gone (similar to locking the stable door after the horse had bolted). Later, in April of the same year, perhaps after the Mayor had calmed down, the gate was shut at night and opened in the day.

1596 [Tomatoes introduced to England.] No toll taken for corn coming into the city due to the famine and high prices.
1597 'Curiously wrought ornamental spire' at White Friars used by sailors as a landmark, demolished.
1599 A grant is given to build the water storage tower on top of the bridgegate at rent of 5^s per annum. Midsummer giants not to parade. Bull ring at cross taken up.
1601 Weir breaks, Dee Mills dry from February until May.
1603 'Tudor House' built (date 1503 is an error). 812 people die from plague. High Cross regilded.
1604 Cathedral bell made (oldest remaining).

locksmiths

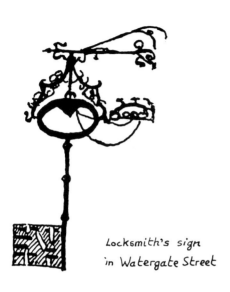

Locksmith's sign
in Watergate Street

The oldest locksmithy still working in Britain
dates from around 1595 and was owned by
John Powell. John Woods, a whitesmith took
over the business in the early 20th century.

An Invoice from 1595

A note of worke done for the use of the Castill by
appointment of Mr James, Connstabell of the Castell,
the second day of December 1595 of me Edward
Powell 1595

Imprimis for meninge A Locke for the castill gate   viij^d (8^d)
Item for mendinge a Locke for A kitchen door   vj^d (6^d)
Item for menddinge A hammer for the use of the keper vj^d
Item for mendinge a borket with my own iron   vj^d
Item for making a resettes for a pear bouttes   iiij^d
Item for mending a tow pear a shakels   x^d
Item for making a new key in the queens bach
within the castil   iiij^d

The medieval and
inappropriately named
'Agricola Tower' at the
castle.

101

The Prospect of Chester, the southwest side — on Hollar's map of 1653.

A tale of two towers

In 1600/1 permission was given to John Tyrer to build a 'Tower or mount over and upon the Bridge gate' with 'Ingins and instruments for the raising forcing or conveying of water from the said Ryver of Dee'. A visitor's account around 1636 states 'wee tooke an exact view of the rare waterworks, which are Middletoniz'd, and brought up to a high Tower, on top of the Gate house, and from thence convey'd by Trunkes and pipes, all the City over.'

John Speed's map of 1610, extract.

John Speed's map, Hollar's map and 'prospect' and Randle Holmes' sketch all show the square, central water tower atop the Bridge Gate.

However, a list of buildings destroyed in the Parliamentarian siege of the city in the Civil War includes '16 The Water Tower, at Dee Bridge'.

Daniel Defoe, in his 'Tour Thro the Whole Island of Great Britain', tells us about the problems: ' 'When I was formerly in the city, about 1690, they had no water to supply their own ordinary occasions but what was carried from the

River Dee upon horses in great leather vessels like a pair of baker's panniers... But, at this time, I found a very good water-house in the river, and the city plentifully supplied by pipes, just as in London is from the Thames.' In between his two visits, in 1692, the Assembly had granted permission for new 'works' to John Hadley and John Hopkins, who had bought Tyrer's grant and a corn mill on the Dee. It would appear that they completely rebuilt the tower to an octagonal design on one side of the bridgegate.

Randle Holmes' sketch of c1640.
Detail of the square tower is shown.

The waterworks did not only supply drinking and washing water. The fire regulations of 1709 order that 'Upon notice of any ffire by the Ringing of the ffire bell in this City the Owners of the Waterworks be obliged to cause their Water Engine on the River Dee to be work'd with the utmost fforce, and the water to be directed as much as may be to the place where such ffire shall happen to be.' The engine in the river was probably an undershot wheel driving a crank and piston.

The setup is made a little clearer in a 1731 coroners' account for the clerk of the waterworks who 'stood upon a plank in the water engine in order to oyl the brasses there he accidentally slipped and fell down headlong under the crank belonging to the said water engine by which fall he received a mortall wound or was crushed and bruised by the said crank in such a barbarous manner that he instantly dyed.'

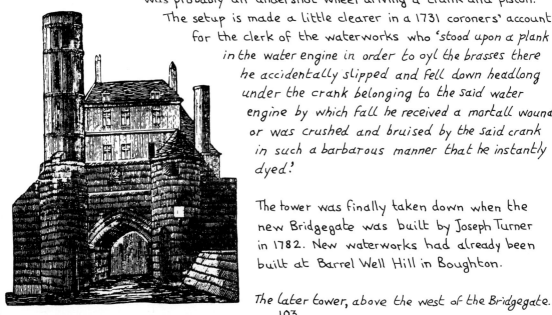

The tower was finally taken down when the new Bridgegate was built by Joseph Turner in 1782. New waterworks had already been built at Barrel Well Hill in Boughton.

The later tower, above the west of the Bridgegate.

103

Cockpit

'In the moneth of ffeabruary 1619 was beganne to be buylded and made a new cocke pitt in a Certayne Crofte neare unto St. John's Church & near to the water syde at the Charges of the Righte honorable Willm Earle of darbye... The Game of Cockfeightinge, at the place before written beganne the sixte day of march 1619 and did Contynue one wholl weeke where at was verye many honorable men & knights and gentlemen at that same game of Cocke feightinge.'

It was this thatched cockpit that was rebuilt with a slate roof in 1825 when five shillings was charged for entry. The 'main' of the fighting season was held here on Races day. Once, when the cockfighting did not finish on time, a message was sent to hold up the race meeting until after the main had finished.

Cockfighting had become fashionable in the reign of Edward III. By the 18th century most grammar schools in England had a yearly fight. Prescott's diary records that in February 1709/10 he gave 'Harry 5s, Ken ½ a Crown, Will 1s for the Cock mony.' At the King's School, in 1754, every boy had to give his master half-a-crown (2s6d) to supply birds. However, Prescott also saw 'in Eastgate Street the barborous divercion of throwing at a Cock notwithstanding applicacion to the Mayor to prevent it'. The exhortations must have taken effect, for the Precedent Book states: 'Whereas Diverse Idle and dissolute people have usually made a Custom on throwing at Cocks... which has been much complained of and abhorr'd... all persons to refrain from the Barbarous practices..'

By 1849 it was the barbarous practice of cockfighting that was made illegal.

Cockpit at Upton-by-Chester

IN THE DOCK

The consistory or ecclesiastical court at Chester Cathedral has the only complete example of this type of court furniture surviving in Britain. Together with its 'apparitor's' (clerk's) seat, it dates from 1635. However, a court existed before that and was situated in the Lady Chapel. It was here, in 1555, that George Marsh, a widower with children, was accused of heresy and preaching Luther's doctrine. He was condemned to death and led to Gallows Hill in Boughton reading his bible, where he was burned at the stake.

1607 New gallery built at Roodee.
1608 Wolfgate rebuilt.
1609 Three 'Saint George's Bells' and a vase used as prizes in races.
1612 Date on beam in 'Coach and Horses'. St Peter's clock strikes quarters.
1613 Companies of Painters etc and Barber Surgeons etc ask to repair Phoenix Tower. Musician George Collie asks that he and fellows be 'waits' of the city. Figs 1/- per lb, sugar 2/1 per lb, strong beer bottles 4d each.
1614 Apprentice innkeeper refused admission as Freeman – innkeeping not suitable trade.
1615 Bishop Lloyd's House (western part) built.

105

However, the consistory court was usually used for petty offences such as pew disputes (heated arguments over the right to seating) thefts and recusancy (more heated arguments but this time from those who didn't even want a pew). There were also cases of working or selling ale on the Sabbath or during divine service. In 1592 Richard Sponne was found guilty of 'keeping horses in the Churchyard & the same unclenlie kept'.

Matrimonial disputes were common. For adultery those supplicants who attended nearly all admitted their faults and were given penances, often to confess in public at their parish church. In many cases, and perhaps to the benefit of the court and offender, this was commuted to a monetary fine.

Other cases included libel. In a 1582 case, Margery Barlow accused Richard Clough of calling her a whore, and her husband Rolfe a stinking cuckoldy knave. Insults were not restricted to Shakespearian times: a similar trial occurred in 1716 when Mary Haliwell accused Elizabeth Edwards of calling her a hairy Hermaphrodite.

An early expression of the tabloid press is seen in the Chronicle of 8th June 1899, which gives a full page to "Charges against the Rector of Nantwich" and his "Alleged immorality with a married lady". The "sensational revelations" were all revealed for the readers although the later result of the trial does not appear to have been as obviously interesting and was not printed.

In the mid-19th century the court lost the right to try cases of libel, matrimonial disputes, loss of tithe and probate cases. Most of the rulings thereafter were about church furniture although in 1971 the chancellor refused permission to open a vault in Gawsworth Church to establish whether Mary Fitton, possibly Shakespeare's 'Dark Lady', was buried there.

CIVIL WAR

The city's loyalty to King Charles I meant great hardship for the citizens. In the build-up to the Civil War a watch was kept at night as early as September 1640. Two years later, and two weeks before King Charles raised his standard at Nottingham, Sir William Brereton, a Cheshire MP, tried to raise men and arms for Parliament at the Cross. The staunchly Royalist mayor had Brereton's men imprisoned and Brereton exiled; Brereton's house, on the site of the former St Mary's Nunnery, was burnt to the ground.

A few weeks later the Assembly assessed a tax of 100 marks on the citizens to repair the walls in a time of 'present and imminent dangers'. The King visited in September and was given 100 lbs of gold. Three hundred citizens were armed with muskets. Yet another £100 was levied on the inhabitants the following February to extend fortifications 'that wee shall all joyne together in a mutuall Associacion for the defence of this Citty'.

Defences around the city and suburbs included this cannon way – Rocky Lane off Parkgate Road.

Ready...   Aim...

Fire!   Sealed Knot reenact the battle 350 years

Sir William Brereton, now in charge of the Cheshire Parliamentary forces, made his first attack in July 1643 but soon retreated to the safety of Tarvin; the city had lost two of its youths, shot dead on the walls. In December more of the city's silver plate was melted to pay for defences as enemy forces encircled the city. Lead from the Cathedral roof was melted down to give to the enemy - fired at them as musket shot. Only a few months later the city was relieved by Prince Maurice. Prince Rupert visited the city and made Lord Byron governor.

However, by the end of the year the siege was resumed in earnest and the King's relief army diverted to Naseby. By May 1645 there was 'no fresh meate and little fish' within the walls. Camped outside, it was little better for the Parliamentary forces who had been scouring the English and Welsh countryside for supplies. Brereton himself was accused of letting his army loot and he had to return to London to answer charges. While he was away, Parliament's forces broke through the eastern suburb's defences, surprising the mayor - who in his hurry to flee left his mace, and his wife! The Parliamentary army started to fire cannon at the east wall of the city.

The King and his army advanced to relieve Chester but they were attacked from front and sides, broke ranks and fled, some for Wales and the rest for the safety of the city.

THIS STONE BALL FOUND EMBEDDED IN ONE OF THE OAK BEAMS WITHIN THE BOOT INN DURING ITS RESTORATION IN 1986 IS A 'HOME MADE' PIECE OF AMMUNITION WHICH MAY HAVE BEEN USED IN A SMOOTH - BORE MUSKET IT COULD BELONG TO THE CIVIL WAR PERIOD BUT IT MIGHT ALSO BE MUCH LATER HAVING BEEN USED BY POACHERS ETC.

Musket shot from the Boot Inn. As the inn was rebuilt during the war it is possible that timbers from demolished houses in the suburbs were used.

1640 Easter Tuesday race replaces traditional Sheriff s' breakfast archery competition. City watch continued through night in 'these warlike and dangerous' times.
1642 [King Charles raids Parliament.]
1643 Sir Wm Brereton attacks city.
1644 Lord Byron made Royalist governor.
1645 King Charles watches his army defeated. He leaves for Wales.
1646 Hunger and starvation - city surrenders to Parliament.
1647 2032 die of plague in 23 weeks.
1649 King Charles proclaimed traitor.
1650 [First coffee house in England at Oxford.] 'Nine Houses' built.
1651 Ten Chester people executed for writing to Charles II.
1652 God's Providence House built.

The remains of the field hospital for the Battle of Rowton Moor.

King Charles watched from the Phoenix Tower as the fighting reached the suburbs, his captain beside him killed by a musket ball after he moved to the Cathedral Tower. Over 600 men died and a further thousand taken prisoner. There was now little chance of saving the city and the King left with 500 troops, but Brereton wrote 'The besieged in Chester remain obstinate'

1656 Three 'witches, hanged after the Michaelmas assizes, are buried by the castle ditch in St Mary's churchyard
1657 First Chester to London coach.
1658 Owen Jones dies leaving charity bequests.
1659 'A great fish the length of 3 yards was taken upon the Sands in Saltney.'
1662 Bowling green made in Cathedral old orchard.
1664 Bridgegate Tavern (now the Bear & Billet) built or rebuilt.
1665 Linencloth market held in Watergate Street Row South. [Plague kills nearly 70,000 Londoners.]
1678 Mayor orders that the Midsummer Show never again be observed in the city.

His mortar attacks 'were great grenadoes like so many demi-phaetons threaten to set the city if not the world alight.' By Christmas, with the city completely encircled and having refused to surrender nine times, Lord Byron having only spring water and boiled wheat for lunch, and many of the citizens resorting to eating their dogs, the city entered into a treaty. On 3rd February Parliamentary forces marched through the open gates. Virtually all the houses outside the walls had been destroyed, either for defence or by attacks, including Bache Hall, Blacon Hall and Hoole Hall. The mills and the waterworks lay in ruins and not one house 'from the Eastgate to the middle of Watergate Street' had escaped bombardment.

The Phoenix Tower became King Charles' Tower in the
19th century.

Phoenix stone on 'King Charles Tower'

Phoenix

On the 30th July 1613 Aldermen and Stewards of the Company of Barber Surgeons, Tallowchandlers and Wanchandlers, and of the Company of Painters, Glaziers, Embroiderers and Stationers stated that they had long been tenants of a stone tower on the City Walls at an annual rent of 2 shillings but, as the roof was 'uncoered with leade and rayne discending upon and into the same', they said it would soon be in ruins if not repaired. They asked the Assembly to retain the current rental fee and let them repair it. Further repairs were done in 1620: 'Pay⁴ to Moses Dalby for mending the glasse windoes of the meeting house 6ˢ8ᵈ.'

Extracts from the accounts of the Stationers' Company show: 'Given to a berrage for severall works about the Phenix for Midsomer Show 18ᵈ' and 'To three men for carrieng the phenix, and for leadinge the horse 18ᵈ.' At the annual guild meeting on the Festival of St Luke in October the tower was decorated with garlands of flowers and the upper floor strewn with rushes.

During the Civil War the guild met in Randle Holmes'(II) house in Watergate Street while the tower was used for 'ordnance' (sic), probably a small gun emplacement. In 1645 King Charles I, as mentioned earlier, watched as his army was driven from Rowton Moor and fighting took place in the suburbs 'from whence he removed to St Werburgh's steeple, where as he was talking with a captaine, a bullet from St John's gave him a salute narrowly missing the King, hit the said captaine in the head, who died in the place. The tower was ruined in the war and rebuilt in 1658.

It was not until 1692/3 that the Phoenix carving was put up and Randle Holmes (Ⅲ) was paid: 'for ye stone which stands over ye phoenix doore 00 18 00 Paid Edward Nixon towards ye putting it up 00 06.' The murengers (wall keepers) were ordered to view and repair the Phoenix tower in 1774. A Mr John Hickson Henshall applied for permission to lease the tower and turn it into a dwelling house in 1818 but the application was rejected. However a use was found for the tower in 1854 when Mr Benjamin Huxley rented the top floor as an observatory at a rent of 2/6 per annum.

Below the tower, beside the canal towpath, are a set of 'pudlocks' designed to hold up wooden scaffolding or 'put ups'? A set dating to the 13th century can be found in Caernarvon Castle but it is not known whether these come from that period. Alternatively they may have been used for 'the quarry near the Phoenix Tower' mentioned in 1711 or perhaps for ramps when cutting the canal in the late 18th century.

BISHOP LLOYD'S PALACE

During the Civil War it was unsafe to meet in the Phoenix Tower which was being used for ordinance or small arms so the Painters, Stationers, Glaziers, Embroiderers and Stationers Company had to meet in the house of Randle Holmes (II) in Watergate Street. There is a phoenix above the enormous fireplace in the eastern part of Bishop Lloyd's Palace, leading a city guide to suggest that this may have been the house referred to in company minutes. However, a plan in the notes of historian Thomas Hughes, who had studied the deeds (now lost), indicates that it was the house to the west of Bishop Lloyd's that was owned by Randle Holmes in 1660.

The bishop was George Lloyd, Bishop of Chester. He died in 1615, the year that the western part of the house was built. He was formerly the Bishop of Sodor and Man, which explains the Legs of Man on the carved front. The three horses' heads are the arms of the Lloyd family.

Biblical scenes include Adam and Eve, Cain and Abel, and Abraham about to sacrifice his son Isaac.

Thomas Hughes states that the building was formerly two houses, the western building owned by an alderman until 1660 when Lady Kilmorey bought it for £450 and the dilapidated eastern one for £44.

The hearth tax returns for 1664/5 show 'Lady Ellinor Kelmory' rated for 16 hearths in St Martin's Ward and this may include another house in the street. In 1705 the house was leased to another alderman.

A sale in 1869 described the eastern part as 'Dwelling House used as a Beer House ... with large room over the beerhouse.' The whole property was known as 'Bishop Lloyd's House'. The building was saved from exportation to America in the late 19th century and was rebuilt in 1899 by Thomas Lockwood. It is now the headquarters of the Chester Civic Trust, for whom it has become a 'palace'.

Opposite: Engraving by W. Batenham 1826.

High Cross

Parliamentary ordinance of 28th August 1643 called for 'the utter demolishing... of all monuments of superstition or idolatry'. However when, after the Siege of Chester, the Article of Surrender, number 10, stated that 'no Church within the City, Evidences or Writings belonging to the same shall be defaced', the citizens may have thought that their central religious monument would remain unscathed.

They were wrong. The Cross was pulled down. The figures, probably of saints, apostles and the Virgin Mary were taken. Three years after surrender, Charles I was proclaimed traitor at 'the cross' although only the base remained.

The Cross head (reconstruction).

The Cross base is still at Plas Newydd in Llangollen.

In 1704/5 the base was removed but on 22nd January a local worthy and diarist, Henry Prescott, asked the mayor to retrieve the square cross stone. Then, on 31st January, he wrote, "The stone is return'd in the Night, the Town surpris'd various and comical conjectures past (sic) at the place."

Sections of the Cross were found hidden under the steps of St Peter's Church in 1806 and it was reerected at Netherleigh House for a period. The base and part of the shaft were given to the famous 'Ladies of Llangollen' in about 1817 and set up in their garden at Plas Newydd. In 1949 the Cross, with new parts, was reconstructed in the Roman Gardens then finally brought back to the city centre in 1975. It has been a meeting place for residents and visitors alike for over six hundred years, the name remaining even when the Cross itself was not there.

Mr Foster reconstructing the Cross in the Roman Gardens during 1949

The High Cross was first mentioned in 1377. In 1461 the city pillory beside it was replaced at the cost of a mark. The Cross was regilded in 1529. It is dressed in May.

Plague

Detail
from a woodcut.

The plague had hit Chester hard over several years.
The medieval Black Death of 1361 and 1369 had severely cut the population. There were plagues in the early 17th century and, after the Civil War, probably due to the conditions of the citizens during the long siege, plague broke out again. During 1647 and 1648 over 2,000 citizens died and grass grew in the streets.

Assembly records give details of the problems early in the seventeenth century. Minutes for September 1602 show that the fair was to be cancelled in view of the outbreak in London, and contributions were to be made to poor families in the city already infected. On the 20th January following it was reported that 'diverse lewde and evyll disposed persons for their own private gaine have carryed about diverse clothes, apparrell and other goodes of persons deceased... of the plague... counstables... ymmediately... shall cause the wearinge apparell and beddclothes... to be ... burned.' However, valuable clothes were to be buried for a season then washed, scoured and cleaned. By October 1603 further attempts at quarantine were being made: since the inhabitants of Upton had always buried their dead in the 'Greene Church yarde' of the Cathedral, the Assembly gave permission that all persons dying of the plague could be carried into the city the usual way until they came to a brick wall adjoining the house of a late alderman. It would be lawful to pull down this small wall to get access to the churchyard, thus avoiding the streets.

Detail from a
woodcut showing
a funeral
procession with
white rods.

The plaque stone once stood opposite the War Memorial in Upton and is now in Church Lane. Money for goods was put in vinegar in the stone to try and stop the spread of the disease.

1679 Father John Plessington hanged drawn and quartered for High Treason under Titus Oates Act.
1683 More ships built in Chester than in Liverpool.
1684 Site of St Giles' Hospital (burnt down in Civil War) granted to the city by Charles II.
1685 'Old House' in White Friars built.
1687 Assay marks on silver: maker's stamp, city arms, city crest and year letter.
1696 101,660 ounces of coin minted at Chester with a 'c' under the monarch's head.
1698 Exchange (town hall) opens. A snuff mill on the Dee.
1700 New bowling green at Cow Lane mentioned in Assembly minutes.

Persons so dying were to be buried at 6pm and each of the persons burying them to carry a 'white rodde'. When leaving they were not to go into any Chester house or converse with the city inhabitants.

Other towns were just as worried. The town council at Ruthin wrote to ask for certificates of freedom from infection for any Chester resident visiting at the 'tyme of our fayre now approaching' and were later extremely annoyed when they found that tradesmen from infected houses had managed to get such certification.

In Chester those infected were moved outside the walls to near the Water Tower. St Peter's Parish records show 'xx^d (20^d) was paid to Bedforde, clerk of St Peter's, for making up the accomptes (accounts) for the collections for the cabins which were built at the water side, near the new tower and in the quarries without the Wall, for the isolation of the infected.' Burials caused other problems: 'paid for v pounds of pitch to perfume the churche after the buryall of Widowe Tropp for she died of the sickness viij^d (8^d)'.

In July 1625 rules were brought into force that: no stranger was to live in the city unless he had not been in London or other infected place for a month – a sworn oath on the New Testament was required. Strangers were not allowed in the city on the pretence of passing through (except by licence) and goods from London were not to be received.

No fairs were held in 1631 or 1636 when wares had to be stored outside the city for a month and any porter viewing the goods was not admitted for a month.

Although some preventative measures may have slowed the spread of the disease, which was carried by fleas on rats, others had little effect. Bernard Wall, a local historian, tells of the mayor who built a new house in the country facing east with no windows on the south side, so that no infected air from London be let in.

Old engraving of God's Providence House.

Built in 1652 and rebuilt in the mid-19th century, God's Providence House is said to have had its motto 'God's providence is mine inheritance' put up by a family who escaped the plague.

However, it is also the motto of the earl of Cork and appears on other houses in England.

NINE HOUSES

Nine almshouses, consisting of four mirrored pairs and an endhouse, were built here in 1650. This design of a solid wall base and timber uppers is rare outside Chester and is more often seen when the wooden base has rotted and been replaced with stone or brick.

Robert Harvey of the City of London, haberdasher, sold all nine to Randle Stanway of Chester for £230. In 1850 numbers 2 and 4 were rebuilt as one house. Two houses were demolished. The remaining six were restored in 1969.

In his book 'Picturesque Chester' Peter Boughton writes that residents of the original almshouses had to be over 65 years old and abstain from tobacco and alcohol.

Glovers' Stone

The bluestone in Water Tower Gardens.

c1700 John Pemberton built the ropewalk at the northwestern corner of the walls. Pemberton's Parlour, semi-circular tower named after him. Stocks put up at the Cross.
1701 Salmon 'mylvell ray or any other sea fish' to be sold at the King's Fishboard on Watergate Street. Citizens could buy 'before 9am, fishmongers after. 'Foreign' fishers could only retail after 10am.
1704 Ordered 'when any Oysters shall hereafter be brought to this city for sale that as soon as Mr Mayor...hath received his Toll (being a hundred Oysters out of every Boat Load) the Owners ... market without paying any further Toll'.

In Chester's Great Charter of 1506 from Henry VII, lands exempted had included 'our castle and our liberty within the boundary commonly called Gloverstone'.

In 1652 the glovers' stone, which may once have been a wet-glover's workblock, was said to be 'a grey stone of marble standing in the street' or a 'blewe marble stone'. It was the recognised boundary marker between the city and the township of Gloverstone which had at its hub the old castle with the shire headquarters.

Daniel King, in 1651, stated that 'The Thieves and Fellons are arraigned in the said Shire-Hall, and, being condemned, are by the Constable of the castle or his Deputy, delivered to the Sheriffs of the city, a certain distance without the castle-gate, at a Stone called, The Glovers Stone: from which place, the said

Sheriffs convoy them to the place of Execution, called Boughton.'

Another source states that petty criminals or vagabonds were
    nded over 'att glovers stoune to such officer of the Cittie of
Chester, in and from hence to whipp them through the Citie.'

When the Mayor visited the castle, he 'put downe the sword ymediately
after he was passed the mere called the glovers stone.'

The area around Bunce Lane, at the junction of Castle Street, where
the glovers' stone stood was also used as a meeting place. In 1666 a
letter went out on behalf of King Charles II to the various hundreds:

> 'Gentlemen
> There being [no] great reason to doubt that there are
> preparations made by Enemies of this Kingdome towards
> an Invasion, Wee cannot omitt to give you Notice thereof,
> you being equally concerned with vs in such a danger.
> And further to Informe you that wee have thought fitt
> to secure this County in the best manner wee can:
> ffor which purpose wee have appointed a meeting at
> Glover Stone upon Tuesday the 17th of this Instant
> July...'

In 1661 the Guild of Barbers Surgeons recorded a charitable gift: 'Given at
the Glovers stone to the Castle Prisoners   6d '

There were also other 'bluestones' in the city apparently used as boundary
stones. It is unknown when they arrived in the area and they may be
reused Celtic stones. The name of Boughton may come from 'bochtuneston'
referring to a bluestone that stood at Spital.

The bluestone in the Water Tower Gardens may be the Glovers' Stone
which, in turn, may be a lost Celtic memorial standing stone.

Owen Jones

THE CITY ARMS

When Owen Jones, a butcher, died in the late 17th century, he bequeathed his land to the 'poor of every Company of Merchants and Craftsmen of Chester.'

The charity flourished when vast quantities of lead ore were mined on the site during the 18th and 19th centuries.

In 1718 his portrait was painted on a wainscot panel inside the old Pentice.

You won't find the City Arms on a pub crawl of Chester. It is on the land bequeathed by Owen Jones, 14 miles away, at Minera. Land sold at Minera and New Brighton included four parcels sold for pubs in the growing mining community.

Inscribed memorial to Owen Jones on the bank beside the Eastgate. The building was built by the charity commissioners.

St Michael's Rectory

The Rectory

Sir Francis Gamul, mayor in 1635, built the small, neat little house in Bridge Street for his daughter, Lettice, in 1659. She bequeathed it, in 1721, to St Michael's Parish 'to augment the stipend of the vicar' and it was used as a rectory. The parish sold it, in 1907, to a Mr Crawford.

In 1975, under Ellis Barker Fur and Fashions, it was restored. The facade was pulled down and contractors found carvings in the original wood which had been covered up to hide the rot. Local craftsmen copied this in the rebuilding and it received an award from the Civic Trust in European Architecture Heritage Year.

During 1998 an interesting exhibition of Chester building models was installed in an upstairs room (see page 234).

Panels of biblical scenes in the row level shop.

bear & billet

The Bear & Billet,
Lower Bridge Street.

The building still contains the granary doors set under the eaves, and many of the 1620 panes of glass it had a century ago. Inside is a modern wall painting of the Mary Rose, Henry VIII's lost battleship. The pub's present name, the Bear and Billet, comes from the heraldic arms of Richard Nevil, Earl of Warwick (1428-71) mentioned in Shakespeare's Henry IV Part 2 Act 5.

It was 1584 when George Talbot, earl of Shrewsbury, inherited part of the sergeancy of the Bridgegate; the townhouse alongside was owned by the Talbot family until 1867 and was leased as a pub from at least the 17th century. In 1664, after damage in the Civil War, this building was rebuilt as the Bridgegate Tavern, the tolls having been sold to the council. Ten years later charges were 'for a waggon load of goods 8^d, horseload or pack 4^d, every beast sold 1^d, parcels carried by porters 1^d; 15 days before or after either fair – double duty.'

In 1710 Thomas Williams, innholder applied for a new lease of the pub, now known as The Bear Inn, and the right to collect tolls at the Bridgegate. He was granted tolls on goods over the value of £12 only. The pub was later known as the Lower White Bear.

Bear and bull baiting was once a popular 'sport' in Chester as in other English cities. In the yearly bull-bait at the Cross it is said that the crier shouted 'Oyez, oyez if any man stand within 20 yards of the bull ring let him take what comes.' The puritan mayor, Henry Hardware, caused 'the bull ringe at the high crosse to be taken up' during his term of office in 1599-1600 but it was soon replaced and official bull-baits continued until 1754 when the mayor and other officials absented themselves.

The Improvement Act of 1762 forbade anyone to 'cause any Bull, Bear, Badger or other Beast to be baited, or worried in any of the streets, Rows or Squares... not exceeding Five Pounds nor less than Five Shillings,' but bull-baits continued outside the walls until 1803.

On at least two occasions bears that had been used as mascots for regiments at the castle were sold to local butchers when they died.

Nowadays it is only teddy bears that can be found in Chester streets.

FOR THE GROWTH OF THE HAIR.

CAUTION.—The great demand for the above article having occasioned numerous Imitations some of which are only mixtures of strong rancid Fats, with pungent essential Oils, and are extremely deleterious. The public are therefore respectfully informed, that the above is now sent out with the words " ATKINSON'S BEAR'S GREASE FOR THE HAIR," burnt on the cover of the pot (not a printed label) is enclosed in a wrapper with his signature and address. The lowest price pot is 2s. 6d. It is now duly established in public estimation, its regenerating properties being universally admitted to a demonstration.

J. A. will only add, that independent of making the Hair grow, it is very pleasant for dressing, making it beautifully soft and glossy. Sold by the Importer, 44, Gerrard-street, Soho-square, London ; and in Chester, by Mr. Bowden, No. 10, and Mr. Duboc, No. 8, Bridge-street-row, and Mrs. Monk, printer, Newgate-street, and most perfumers. Price in pots, 2s. 6d. and 4s. and in bottles, 3s. 6d. and 7s. 6d. Perfumed with Otto of Roses, extra price.

Advert from Chester Chronicle, June 1826 CR655/7

Silver

Imports of lead from North Wales for export started early in the Roman occupation. One lead ingot found in Wales, from about AD60, was marked with the name Nipius Ascanius, even before the legions took Wales. With the lead mineral ore, Galena, came silver, present at the rate of about 0.5%.

In Saxon times over a hundred moneyers struck coin in the city over the years with the letters LEGE, or similar, to represent LEGECEASTER (Chester). The Domesday book records that there were 'seven moneyers in the city' when the Normans conquered. The mint here was continued until 1154.

During 1406/7, three goldsmiths were taken to the Crownmote court for charging excessive fees and not paying customs. The Goldsmiths' Company was established in 1475/6. By the 16th century there was a demand for civil plate for ceremonial functions as well as silver church plate and cups in Cheshire and North Wales parishes. Between 1550 and 1650 there were about 30 goldsmiths in the city. At Shrovetide, after 1540, a silver cup had to be made for the races and 'gleaves' (silver arrows) for some of the other guilds to give as prizes.

During the Civil War hundreds of pounds worth of the city's silver plate was melted down and turned into coin to pay for costly defences.

Perhaps to boost their numbers, the goldsmiths joined their guild to the watchmakers after the war, in 1665.

A lead ingot found on the Roodee may have fallen from a ship being loaded in the Roman port which was situated there. With the lead ore came silver.

As part of his uniform the city bellman had a silver badge while, during the late 17th century, almsmen from St John's Hospital had to wear silver badges (probably on their arms) with the name of their benefactor, at least for formal occasions. Many of these still survive and are on display in the Grosvenor Museum silver collection.

A mint was opened at the castle and, between the years 1696 and 98 when it operated, silver weighing 46,216 Kilos was pressed into coin.

A Chester shilling minted in 1697. Note the 'C' under the king's head

In 1687 an assay office had been opened. The word 'assay' comes from the French 'assai' – to test. In the 'refiner's fire' used since pre-Roman times it is possible to obtain the 'noble' metals. By adding lead then heating in a bone-ash cupel, the unwanted metals oxidise and the liquid is soaked into the porous cupel until only pure gold, silver or

platinum is left. Grains were taken from silverwork to test. On the assayed product each goldsmith had to register his mark. Silverwork was also dated with Gothic capitals: 'A' for the first year, 'B' for the next etc.

At the Chester assay office the other two 'punsons' were the old city arms and the city crest. However, after 1696 all Brittania standard silver had to be assayed in London, leaving Chester goldsmiths in limbo. This unwarranted state of affairs did not last for long and in an Act of 1701 some assay offices, including Chester, were authorised. A continuous sequence of letters was now used. From 1720 a Lion passant and a leopard's head were included as stamps on Chester silver.

 Chester City Arms, Hallmark 1701–79.

 Chester Hallmark before 1701 and after 1779.

 Lion Passant.

The late 19th century saw watchcases from Liverpool and Birmingham assayed here as well as art silver. George Lowe, who had been admitted to the goldsmiths in 1791, was made assay master in 1840 after fraudulent dealings by the former master. Lowe & Sons shop can still be found in Bridge Street Row. The assay office closed in 1962 although the original assay office is part of Goldsmiths in Eastgate Street Row.

Left and overleaf: Modern silverware made in Chester. Colin Smith's modern work depicting shells and sea creatures is stamped with the Chester mark and can be found in Lowe's.

BLUECOAT HOSPITAL

'Whereas it is evident to common observation that the growth of vice and Debauchery is greatly owing to the gross Ignorance of the Principles of the Christian Religion, especially among the poorer sort and Whereas Christian Virtue can grow from no other root than Christian Principles; we whose names are Underwritten, being touched with zeal for the Honour of God, and the Salvation of Souls, and the promoting of Christian Knowledge do hereby promise to pay yearly during Pleasure by four equall payments at Candlemas, May Day, Lammas and All Saints, such respective sums as we hereto subscribed for and towards setting up a school within the City of Chester for teaching poor boys (whose Parents can afford them no education to read and write, and cost Account, and to repeat and Understand the Church Catechisms according to the Rules and orders to be agreed upon by the Subscribers for the Management of the said school.'

Founded in 1700, the Bluecoat was the first 'Society for the Promotion of Christian Knowledge' charity school outside London. Nicholas Stratford (1633-1707) Bishop of Chester 1689-1707 was a signatory to the first constitution of the SPCK on the 19th April 1699. In 1704 it was ordered that £3 a year should be paid out of the city treasury towards the maintenance of the 'poor blew coat boys in this Citty.' Stratford died in 1707 and finally, in 1717, the Hospital was built on a site donated by the Corporation.

Here, Ranulph III earl of Chester had earlier (c1190) founded the Hospital of St John the Baptist for the 'sustentation of poor and silly persons'.

1707 Morgan's Mount rebuilt. Horseraces at Roodee run clock-wise around poles. Three heats of three circuits unless one horse leads heat by 120 yards.

1709 Fire regulations include: ...'no person whatsoever shall lay or keep in any house, Bakehouse or any other place within this city ... any quantity more than Thirty kids at any one tyme of Gorse, Ffurze or Ffaggots...'

1710 Cop built around Roodee. St Michael's tower built above row.

1712 'a dangerous and useless row' at the end of Watergate St opposite Trinity Church closed.

131

&NOTICE.&

WHEREAS some evil disposed persons frequently and wantonly break the Windows of the
BLUE COAT HOSPITAL, by throwing from
the City Walls;

This is to Give Notice,

That a REWARD OF FIVE SHILLINGS
will be paid to any individual giving such information of the Offenders, as shall lead to their
conviction, by application at the School.

Chester, printed by J. Fletcher, Chronicle Office.

1838 notice.   CR 36/31

In 1539 this was referred to as 'the hospitalle
of withoute the Northgate of Westchester'.
Thirteen inmates were given 'a good loaf
daily, a great dish of pottage, a piece of
flesh or fish and a half-a-gallon of
competant ale'.

These buildings were destroyed during
the Civil War to avoid giving shelter
to Parliamentarian attackers, and
shortly afterwards the land was
given to the council, later to become
the Bluecoat Hospital site.

1712 *Last witch execution in England.*
1713 *Fire regulations of 1709 ordered
to be 'writ fair' and posted up
in frame at Pentice include:
'fflaxdressers ... do not smoke
Tobacco ... in their fflax shops'.*
1714 [*D. Fahrenheit makes mercury
thermometer on the Continent.*]
1715 *Wellington stays at Park House.*
1717 *Bluecoat School open.*
1719 *Silver oar made for the mayor as
a symbol of his 'admiral' status.*
c1720 *Recorder's Steps finished.*
1721 *The going rate for 'whipping
a vagrant' by the Beedle was 1/.*
1725 *Riverside groves laid out
with lime trees by Charles
Croughton, Swordbearer
of the city.*

Boys at the boarding school in the Bluecoat Hospital wore blue uniforms and learnt the four 'r's - reading, 'riting, 'rithmetic and religion — from 6am until 5pm. A Green Cap day school was added in 1790. The day school closed in 1901, the boarding school in 1949. Today students from University College have their history department in the Bluecoat.

1727 [First marriage announcement in a newspaper.]
1729 Row at Hope & Anchor in Northgate Street enclosed. North wing of Charity School for 'blew Coat boys' not yet built. Bakers permitted to build windmills at Hough Green.
1731 [10 Downing Street built.]
1733 First sod cut of the canalised Dee.
1739 Great frost, carts crossed the Dee over ice; a sheep roasted on the ice.
1741 Handel plays parts of the Messiah in Chester.
1742 For preventing dangers to the city by fire, no person should burn corkwood in any street.
1745 As a precaution, in the Jacobite rebellion, Watergate and Northgate walled up.

Rear cover photo:
The bluecoat statue was added in 1854 when the building was enlarged and almshouses built in the courtyard. John Coppack was the model for the statue. A shoemaker's son, he became a coal merchant then worked for the Shropshire Union Canal Co. Many of his descendents still live in the area.

Recorder's Steps

The first city recorder is believed to have been Ralph Birkenhead in 1506. He was the chairman of the Quarter Sessions created by Henry VII in his Great Charter that year. Recorders were elected by Assembly until 1832, then by the Crown. The oath of this official was, 'I shalbe true liege man unto the kinges ma'tie and to the Earle of Chester and the same truely mayntayne with all my mighte and power and truely obey my Mayor, for the tyme being, in all

Artwork beside the Recorder's Steps in summer.

things lawfull, and truely occupye the office of Recorder of the Cittye of Chester and all that to the same apperteyneth as helpe me God so.'

It would appear that one recorder not only used his might and power but all his money as well for, in 1694, Benjamin Ratcliffe, the son of John Ratcliffe, late Recorder and 'Parliament man' for the city (recorders had served in Parliament as MPs for a century), petitioned the Assembly.

John Ratcliffe had been elected in 1646. He refused to take the oath of allegiance in 1651, but was reelected in 1656, serving in Parliament for the last time in 1660.

His son's petition was that his father had expended 'such great *sums of money'* in the service of the city that he had been unable to provide for him. As a result the treasurers were ordered to pay Benjamin the sum of £10.

A plaque states that the Recorder's Steps were built by Recorder Roger Comberbach for access to his house in 1700 but this may be liberal with the truth. In 1690 a sum of £3/4/- was spent on *'making a pair of stairs to Mr Comberbach's back room'.* These may have been wooden stairs inside or outside his house. The stone steps probably came later.

As well as being a well-off merchant, Comberbach achieved some fame when he was imprisoned by a colonel in the guardhouse during 1715 because he advised the Mayor to request the colonel's attendance at the Pentice to answer a complaint against him. The colonel was later cashiered.

Comberbach died in 1719 and the steps may date from that time, for in 1720 the Assembly ordered that a bargain be made with the city's mason or any other to make a new pair of stairs between the bridge and Dee Lane. Later the same year it was ordered that any sum not exceeding twenty pounds be lent out of the treasury to the murengers for the new stairs. In March 1720 money was spent to *'level about the stairs'* and £1/18/6 for *'Lime to the new stairs'.* It seems that the so-called Recorder's Steps were actually the *'New Stairs'* and built in 1720.

On 21st May 1721 Kenneth Edwards, a tanner, fell down the *'new stairs'* and died.

The last Quarter Sessions were held in 1971 and now there is only an Honorary Recorder appointed by the city. The last recorder in 1971, Sir Francis Bart Williams QC, was created the first honorary recorder. He died in 1995 and a new honorary recorder, Judge Elgin Edwards was appointed in 1997.

There was once a curtain around the horsetraders' bench in the Boot Inn. Here the traders could discuss their prices in private. When the lights grew low it is said that the 'ladies' discussed their prices here.

Horsetraders' Bench

The Assembly Book minutes for 26th January 1704 record that, 'It is ordered that the horse fair shall be kept for the future in the fforegate street of this City and in no other place, and that publick notice thereof be posted up in due tyme before the next ffair; and that the ffurther Northgate Street be the fixt place for the beast markett: and that the Clothmarket be continued in the Bridge Street where itt now is and not removed to any other place.'

At the horse fair a proclamation would have been shouted by the bellman or crier. This, the only complete local proclamation recorded, can be found in the Precedents Book at the City Record Office:

'The Worshipfull the Sheriffs of this City do will[&]require in his Maj'tys name strictly charge and Command all manner of p'sons that shall resort to this Fair that they be of good Char' & keep the peace as they and every of them will answer the Contrary of their Utmost Perills.

The Worshipfull the Sheriffs of this City do will & require in his Maj'tys name strictly Charge and command all manner of p'sons that shall during this fair Buy sell & exchange [or] otherwise Depart with any Horse Mare Gelding or Colt that they and every [of] them do make their repair to the said sheriffs or to such p'son or p'sons as they shall app'tt to record all such contracts pay Toll for the same upon payn of such Loss and punishm^t as is appointed by the Laws and Statutes of this Realm. God save the King and the Worshipfull the Sheriffs of this City'

The City Record Office also hold the Sheriffs' Books containing details of all horse sales. The earliest surviving example, from May 1655, shows that,

'Will^iam Roberts of Handbridge in the Countie of the Cittie of Chester husbandman hath sould unto Matthew Scott of Dublin gent^leman one sorril bay nagge with three white ffeet and a white face wh'ch ambles price iii^li v^s (£3/5/-)'

1752 New year starts in January for first time. 3rd September becomes 13th September.[Riots by people who believe they lose 10 days.] John Wesley's diary: Sat Jun 20th 'I rode into Chester and preached at the accustomed place, a little without the gates near St John's.' At the beginning of July a mob pulls down the house where he had preached.
1754 Each boy at the King's School pays 2^s6^d for 'cock money' to buy game cocks for sport.
1755 Infirmary opens in Bluecoat.
1756 Last service for Chester minstrels in St John's Church.
1757 White ware pottery produced in Handbridge.

At a respectable Meeting of the Commissioners under the Act of 2d of his present Majesty's Reign, for amongst other things " Regulating the Chairmen within the City of Chester," held at the Exchange Assembly Room in the said City, on Friday the second Day of May, 1800, to take into Consideration the propriety of Advancing the CHAIRMEN'S RATES during the present high Price of Provision :—The following Rates & Rules were ordered to be taken and Observed by the CHAIRMEN plying within the City of Chester, to Commence on Monday the 5th Day of May Instant, and to continue in force until the 24th Day of October next.

TWENTY-ONE COMMISSIONERS PRESENT.

FOR every Set-down within the Distances herein after-mentioned, to wit ; From any part of this City or the Liberties thereof, within the Distances after named :

	£.	s.	d.
To the Extent of the Houses in the further Northgate-street,			
To the Maypole, in Handbridge,			
To Mr Egerton's House without the Bars,			
To any Houses without the Watergate, and within the Crane,	0	0	9
To any Houses by Dee-side, as far as Mrs. Kendrick's Garden,			
Double Fare,	0	1	6
For every Set-down within the Liberties of this City, beyond the above Limits, except the Ellesmere Canal Wharf,	0	1	0
Double Fare,	0	2	0
To or from the Ellesmere Canal Wharf, from or to any part of the City	0	1	6
For waiting the first Hour,	0	1	0
For every Hour afterwards,	0	0	9
From 12 o'Clock at Night to 1 in the morning	0	1	0
From 1 to 2	0	2	0
After 2,	0	3	0

The Hours of waiting to be from nine o'Clock in the Morning untill twelve at Night, at the several Places where the Chairmen usually stand, or at their respective Dwelling-houses.

At all Assemblies, Balls, Plays, or other Public Nights, where the Chairmen attend, they are to range their Chairs in a Line, to take each their Fare in Rotation as they come upon the Stand, and to continue plying until Half an Hour past twelve o'Clock.

The Chairmen cannot engage their Chairs, or keep them in waiting for any particular Person on any of the above Nights.

If a Chair be sent for to any House, and brought at the Time appointed without being used, the person sending for it is to pay Sixpence in lieu of a Fare.

Every Person sending for a Chair and keeping it above a Quarter of an Hour before using it, shall pay a Fare of one Shilling.

The Chairman to attend at any House or Place where desired, and and carry the Person applying for that Purpose, unless they are engaged in carrying any other Person.

The Chairs to be numbered, and the Name of the Foreman to be painted on the Front of each Chair.

Chairman are not to be impertinent, or otherwise mis-behave themselves.†

Taking more than the above Fares, or breaking any of these Rules, subjects the Chairmen to a penalty of Five Shillings, or to suspension for such time as the Commissioners shall think fit.

† By being Drunk, Noisy, &c.

———o———

Chester, Printed by BROSTER & SON, Exchange.

Sedan House

In 1921 a writer to the Cheshire Sheaf told that while 'railways were in their earliest infancy... one of my earliest memories is associated with a row of sedan chairs standing at the Cross on the south side of St Peter's Church while the bearers leaned against the wall of the church, each with a bundle of sticks beside him, from which they appeared to be forever whittling endless vent pegs, for beer barrels, and strewing the footpath with their chips and debris.'

These two-manpower, pole-mounted, covered chair-taxis for one passenger were popular forms of transport during the 17th, 18th and 19th centuries.

In 1820 it was said that, 'the ladies use sedan chairs when they pay formal visits or attend the assemblies or theatre, the gentlemen usually walk.'

Sedan House, near the Watergate, has two doors in the porch so that the sedan passenger could step inside without being affected by adverse weather conditions. The chairmen were not so lucky.

Coach
and
Four

Getting Started
from 'Coaching Days and Coaching Ways'

The first London to Chester coach started in 1657 and was running three times a week by 1673. It took four days for the slow and uncomfortable journey.

Then, in 1706, Henry Mill invented carriage springs. By 1761 the first express coach or 'Flying Machine' to London started from the White Lion in Northgate Street. This new light coach might be shaped like a diving bell or a violin case and was hung, equally balanced, between huge front and rear steel springs. Coaches would have their name and destination painted on the side, an impressive moving advertisement for all to see. Two such, in 1813, were the 'Lord Wellington' and the 'Light Balloon.'

The landlord of the Pied Bull started a four-horse coach from Chester to Birkenhead for the Liverpool Ferry in 1784. Only a year later the Royal Irish Mail's London via Chester to Holyhead coaches ran from the Bull. Fares were Chester to London £3/3/- and Chester to Holyhead £1/11/6.

In 1823, every day from Chester, the 'Favourite' ran to Newcastle, the 'Independent' to Preston Brook, 'Bang-up' to Shrewsbury, 'Dart' to Manchester and 'Regulator' to Liverpool.

The Flying Machines took only two days to London. This haste, which to passengers created the effect of 'a ship rocking or beating against a heavy sea' was bound to cause accidents and it did.

CHESTER and LONDON
POST-COACHES,

With Four Horses and Two Postillions, on a new Plan, and of
an easy and genteel Construction, with Springs.

(To carry Four People in TWO DAYS.)

SETS out (by way of *Whitchurch*, and lie at the *White-Bear Inn*, in *Coventry*) from *White-Lion Inn*, in *Chester*, on *Monday* April the 16th, and will continue to lie the same Inn every *Monday*, *Wednesday* and *Friday*.

And from the *Blossom's Inn*, *Laurence-Lane, London*, the Day at o'Clock each Morning.

And also sets out (by way of *Nantwich*, and lie at the *Yatch Inn*, in *Chester*, on *Tuesday* April the 17th, and Inn, every *Tuesday*, *Thursday* and *Saturday*.

And from the *White-Bear Inn*, in *Piccadilly, London* same Hour. Gentlemen and Ladies paying Three *Chester*, and Fourpence a Mile for any Part of the Road Twenty Pounds Weight of Luggage; all above to pay ness to be Paid at Booking, the other getting into the Coach.

Perform'd (if God permit) by

Dan. Smith, *Chester*.
James Spencer, *Whitchurch*.
William Parks, *Newport*.
William Smith, *Four Crosses*.
James Penn, *Welch Harp*.
Stephen Windam, *Castle-Bromwich*.
------ Thomas, *Coventry*.

John Hart,
William
Thomas L____ oor
James Morgan, *Stone*.
Thomas Butler, *Litchfield*.
William Webster, *Coleshill*.
------ Soden, *Coventry*.

William Berry, *Dunchurch*.
------ Clarke, *Daventry*.
Pratt and Edge, *Towcester*.
------ Forfeit, *Stony Stratford*.
William Powell, *Brickhill*.
Alexander Jeffereys, *Dunstable*.
J__ a Connor, *Barnet*.

N. B. A Bye Coach may be had at any Time to perform in Two, Three, or Four Days, as the Parties shall agree. If any Accident should happen, the Company will be conveyed without Loss of Time, and the Proprietors keep Carriages for Posting. Likewise good Post Horses for Servants.

* The Public will please to observe, the Scheme of this is not to carry any Outside Passengers, or Luggage, but only such Luggage as belongs to those who honour the Proprietors with their Company. Books kept at the *White-Lion* and *Yatch* Inns.

††† The Proprietors will not be accountable for any Jewels, Rings, Watches, Plate, Money, Bank No or Writings, that may be lost, except entered and paid for as such.

☞ A He_____ ng Coach may be had by applying to Mr. *Dan. Smith, Chester*.

R : Printed by ELIZ. ADAMS.

In 1827 the Chester and Holyhead Mail, on turning at the foot of a hill, turned over, crushing Mr Egerton, brother of a Cheshire MP, and throwing the luckier guard into a ditch.

Sometimes the accidents were caused by dangerous driving. A mile from St Albans the Holyhead Mail 'attempted to pass the Chester Mail by galloping furiously by on the wrong side of the road. The coachman of the Chester Mail resented the indignity and pulled his leaders across his rival's — a heap of stones by the side of the road did the rest of the business and in a moment converted two spick-and-span turnouts, full of passengers more or less alive and alarmed, into a mass of struggling horseflesh, splintered wood and groaning wounded... a verdict of manslaughter (for one fatality) was returned against both.'

Racing the Mail
from 'Coaching Days and
Coaching Ways.'

The old coaching sign outside the Pied Bull in Northgate Street states that London is 198 miles but in 1675 John Ogilby recorded it as 182 miles 1 furlong whilst in 1818 a Mr G Steele saw the stone milepost outside the White Lion. It said, 'London 182 miles.'

Highway robbery was only too common so the mail coach carried an armed guard. A newspaper reports one local occasion:

'On Saturday morning last as Andrew Ran, Esq: Knight of the shire for the county of Wexford in the kingdom of Ireland, and his lady were journeying in a post chaise from Parkgate towards this city, at about a mile's distance from the halfway house on the Weston side; a footpad stopped the postillion, and immediately presenting his pistol through the window of the chaise, demanding their money, and robbed them of two purses of gold, and a large gold repeating watch, with some valuable seals. He then produced a pocket common prayer-book and obliged the lady and gentleman to take an oath, and kiss the book, that they would not discover anything related to the present transaction until they arrived at Chester; he then wished them well, civilly took his leave and went over a hedge...'

WILLIAM JONES,

FEATHERS HOTEL, BRIDGE-STREET,
Chester.

From Chester to London 182 Miles.—To Holyhead 90.

From Chester to Manchester...38	From Chester to Conway........50
................Liverpool........17	................Bangor.......65
................Stockport....39	................Wrexham.....12
................Knutsford.....25	................Mold.......12
................Macclesfield ...36	................Ruthin 20
................Shrewsbury ...40	................Denbigh 28
................Oswestry 27	................Ellesmere ...24
................Nantwich 20	................Whitchurch 20
................Northwich 18	................Tarporley 10
................Holywell.....18	................Frodsham 10
................St. Asaph... 29	................Warrington 20
................Abergele.......38	................Parkgate......11

	£.	s.	d.
BREAKFAST			
LUNCH...................			
DINNER			
DESSERT			
TEA and COFFEE			
SUPPER			
WINE........................			
CLARET....................			
MADEIRA....................			
NEGUS and PUNCH.............			
RUM and BRANDY			
GENEVA			
ALE and PORTER			
CIDER, PERRY, and SPRUCE.......			
POP and SODA WATER			
SERVANTS' EATING and BEER......			
HORSES' HAY and CORN			
BEDS and FIRE			
POST CHAISE			
PAPER, TOBACCO, and CIGARS......			
WASHING			
SADDLER and SMITH......			
LETTERS' and PARCELS.............			

£ /

T. GRIFFITH, PRINTER, CHESTER.

Highway robbery carried a death sentence but, during the 18th and 19th centuries, in cases where murder was not committed this could be commuted to transportation to His Majesty's colonies for life.

Bill of fare from the Feathers Hotel, a local coaching inn.
CR 119/23
(The 91 should, of course be 19.)

THE CHESTER
Weekly---Journal;
Being a COLLECTION
OF
The moft Material NEWS
Both Foreign and Domeftick.

Numb. 174. Thurfday September 3. 1724.

Licenc'd and Enter'd in the Stamp-Office.

CHESTER : Printed by Wm. Cooke, where may be had Collectors Warrants, Warrants for the High-ways, and Orders of removals do. Note any Juftices Clerks may be fupply'd by the Men that carry this News

The Chester Weekly Journal traced from the photo of issue 174 with its blurred woodcut, and a copy of the woodcut from issue number 2 held at the Chester Record Office.

THE TABLOID PRESS

Before 1693 printing presses were only allowed in London, Oxford, Cambridge and York. Although Randle Holmes 'Academy of Armour' has Chester on the title page, it is possible that T. Tillier the typographer may have had it printed in London.

In 1688 there is a handbill of William Thropp, a printer, apparently printed in Chester. Early in the 18th century the Stationers' Company recorded payments to travelling printers. It is not clear whether they carried around small presses or took the text to print elsewhere. However, the first recognised city printer was Edward Ince, a freeman of the city in 1709, who printed several books here. His press was purchased by William Cooke who had served his apprenticeship in Dublin. Setting up near the Eastgate as a printer and bookseller, he was soon accused by the Painters, Glaziers, Embroiderers and Stationers' Guild of selling books without permission. Cooke had little choice but to join the company at a fee of £25 in 1727.

It was William Cooke who brought out the first newspaper for the city: the 'Chester Weekly Journal' hit the press in the 1720s. The one remaining photo of issue 174 and the original of issue 2 both date to September of different years, suggesting that Cooke's Weekly Journal was not always weekly. The format changed from a nearly-A4 broadsheet to a smaller-than-A5 tabloid during its short life. Inside was news from London and abroad but only the corn prices from Chester. In 1733 it was followed by the 'Industrious Bee' and Cooke also printed the 'Chester Weekly Tatler' in 1734 when once again he upset the powers that be and was fined £10 for selling it unstamped. There was now, also, some competition: 'Adams Weekly Courant' (note Eliz Adams was the printer of the coach notice on page 143). The Courant came into being in 1732 and became the 'Chester Courant' in 1793. It ceased printing in the early 1980s leaving the 'Chester Chronicle', first published in 1775, as Chester's oldest surviving newspaper. The city also has the 'Chester Evening Leader' and two free papers: the 'Chester and District Standard' and the 'Chester Mail'.

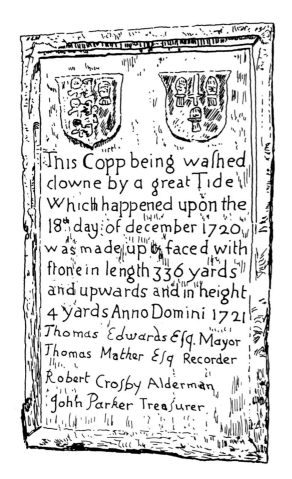

This Copp being washed
downe by a great Tide
Which happened upon the
18th day of december 1720
was made up & faced with
stone in length 336 yards
and upwards and in height
4 yards Anno Domini 1721
Thomas Edwards Esq. Mayor
Thomas Mather Esq Recorder
Robert Crosby Alderman
John Parker Treasurer

The inscribed stone from the Copp was found on the old city workhouse adjoining the Chester Gas Company's new works at the beginning of the 20th century. It was given to the Grosvenor Museum on the 26th January 1904. It can be seen in the museum garden.

Monumental Inscription

Daniel Defoe in his 'A Tour Through the Whole Island of Great Britain' published in 1724-6, records that, 'The walls as I have said, are in very good repair, and within the battlements, from whence you may see the country round; and particularly on the site of the Roodee, which is a fine large low green, on the bank of the Dee. In the winter this green is often under water by the inundations of the river, and a little before I came there, they had such a terrible flood, which flowed 8 foot higher than usual so that it not only destroyed a fine new wharf and landing-place for goods, a little below the town, bore down all warehouses, and other buildings, which the merchants had erected for securing their goods, and carried all away goods and buildings together, to the irreparable loss of the persons concerned.'

Research courtesy of Roy Wilding

graffiti

'Charming Miss Oldfield 1736' can still be found inscribed on a glass pane in Leche House, Watergate Street Row South. Other inscriptions here were 'Barker' 'Miss Wantran' and 'Llewelin Barry.'

Graffiti on windows seem to have been the expression of the day. Thomas Hughes recorded that virtually every pane of glass at Bishop Lloyd's Palace contained an inscription including the following: 'Oh that my Pencil could the features trace Of him I think possessed of every Grace S Pollard' 'Robert Duff Oct 16th 1853' 'JH 1781' 'Sarah and Anne Hurleston 1722' 'Catherine Dale' 'Robert Owens 1751' 'Joan Collins 1775'

It seems that graffiti had no class boundaries for there was also the inscription: 'Watkin Williams Win Mayor of Chester 1727'

When Dean Swift, author of Gulliver's Travels, stayed at the former Yacht Inn in Watergate Street, he invited dignitaries from Chester Cathedral to supper. When none turned up he scratched this little ditty on the window with his diamond ring:

'Rotten without and mouldering within This place and its clergy are nearly akin'

1761 Infirmary moves to north-west quarter of city. Improvement Act orders that 'no person whatsoever shall throw, cast, lay, bring, drive or convey, or cause, permit or suffer to be thrown, set, cast, laid, brought, drove or carried, any Ashes, Rubbish, Soil, Timber, Bricks, Stones, Slates, Coals, Dirt, Dung, Filth, Casks, Tubs, Goods, Merchandize, Coaches, Waggon, Carts or other Carriages or any Annoyance, Nuisance, or Obstruction whatsoever.'

1762 Boughton turnpike erected.

1768 Thomas Boswell petitions to build steps from walls at Abbey Green.

GOLDEN FALCON

Handel, travelling to Ireland in 1741, stayed at the Golden Falcon in Northgate Street for three days, as the wind was unfavourable to embark from Parkgate. He was writing his famous work 'The Messiah' and applied to the Cathedral organist to find choristers who could read 'at sight'. Janson the printer was one of the choir, recommended because of his bass voice; but when it came to practice he consistently failed to sing the correct notes.

Handel, after swearing in four or five languages, cried out in broken English, "You schauntrel, did not you tell me that you could sing at sight?" "Yes Sir," said the printer, "and so I can, but not at first sight."

The Golden Falcon mosaic outside Centurion House, Fireman's Square, Northgate Street.

There was a White Bull Inn mentioned in 'Northgayte Street' in 1642. It lasted until 1752 when it was incorporated into the Golden Falcon. Assembly records show that a Row at the Hope and Anchor, formerly four doors from the Falcon Inn in Northgate Street, was enclosed early the same century.

By 1772 the former row had become a vinegar manufactory. George Eaton bought the property in 1816 from Peter Dutton. Later, Peter Eaton (mayor 1856-7) brewed beer, altered the stables to take more fermenting vessels and had a 33 metre well sunk. In 1849 he was given

The former Northgate Brewery in Northgate Street.

notice by the council to control the smoke of his furnaces. Eaton's Brewery expanded and took over the Kelsterton Brewery and St Winefrede's Brewery at Holywell. In 1864 Henry Ford, Frederick Gunton and William Kelly bought the Eatons out. The Northgate Brewery Company Ltd was formed in 1884. The company had 'Bottling Stores, Wine and Spirit Vaults' at 7 Foregate Street and malt kilns on the east side of Lower Bridge Street. Its popular bitter beer won a first prize in 1928 while the company owned pubs in Cheshire and North Wales, including the Oddfellows Arms in Frodsham Street.

Greenall Whitley, a Warrington based brewery, took over in 1949, closing the Chester site. The area was excavated: the 1973 report of Roman and other finds can be found in the library. Centurion House was built and the Falcon mosaic from the former off-licence doorway put outside its entrance.

1768 Eastgate pulled down. Parts of the Roman gateway found.
1769 Eastgate completed (minus clock). Two stone chairs erected on enlarged racecourse.
1771 45 inward vessels come to Chester up the new cut.
1772 Procession celebrates Chester Canal Act. Strolling players: 'The sons of mirth and humour' give puppet show — 800 lbs of gunpowder stored below explode killing 23.
1773 First city public library.
1774 John Edmon, keeper of the Roodee to be paid 6s weekly and have liberty to collect, one day in each race week, 1s per carriage but he has to do the labourer's work.

149

Blocked up windows in Castle Street.

WINDOW TAX

In Britain there has been a tobacco tax since 1625, an income and property tax since 1642, and there was a local hearth tax until the latter part of the 17th century. Hearth tax was collected half yearly, within 20 days from Michaelmas and Lady Day. Records for the year 1664/5 show that over 40 Chester houses had none of a similar size in Liverpool. John Anderson, a merchant who later became mayor, had 23 hearths compared with the dean's 12. Income tax was set at 10% on earnings over £200 in 1798 to pay for the Napoleonic wars. It was stopped in 1815 but the government could not let sleeping dogs lie and it was resumed in 1842.

A tax collected on windows during the years 1695-1851 was the forerunner of our rates, short-lived poll-tax, and council tax system. An order in the Precedent Book of the council shows that, in the mid-18th century, collectors were '...to collect half a years House and Window duties and a Quarters Land Tax... and to pay the same at the Talbott on Wednesday the 14th day of October next.' The tax led some to fill in as many windows as possible. Take pity, though, on the poor Russians. They had to pay a beard tax in 1698.

From pillar to post

Chester Exchange (town hall)
1698 - 1762

'In 1756 the west side of the Exchange had given way and was likely to fall. Mr Turner, an architect was sent for from Whitchurch to survey it. In consequence the row of large stone pillars was removed from the centre towards the east side and a row of shops built along the west side. In removing the pillars, one which stood at the corner of Mr Broster's shop was broken off at the top end, the corporation made a present of it to the dean and chapter to make an obelisk, to be erected in the centre of Abbey Square where it now stands?

Roman column bases, Roman drains and an 18th century column (whoops!) outside the Library.

A blue plaque in Abbey Square states that the pillar in the former pond came from the Exchange but the original pillar, apart from being broken, also, according to one historian was oval! The pillar in the square is neither oval nor broken (see the photo on page 79) and does not match William Batenham's drawing (see Picturesque Chester, p33).

When a collection of 'Roman' stones was put outside the Library,

151

a pillar was brought from the Water Tower Gardens. The Chief Executive of the council asked the Curator of the Grosvenor Museum for an assurance that it was Roman.

"I can assure you that it isn't", was the reply. This little *faux pas* was soon corrected by a plaque which stated that the tall pillar was Georgian, and the stones, now from very different times, even won an award.

The statue of Queen Anne and a lead cistern from the Exchange were moved to Bonewald-esthornes Tower on the city walls after the Exchange burnt down. Later the statue fell off and was taken away, presumably in bits, by council workmen, never to be seen again.

The old spire of Trinity Church (the present Guildhall) has been moved several times. It was erected in the Infirmary grounds as a base for a sundial and has now appeared in a small garden at the Countess of Chester hospital.

The Victorian postbox outside the Town Hall has not been moved there from somewhere else – it is a replica. A real, but less visually interesting, Victorian postbox, can be found on the bend of St Werburgh Street. There is another in Crook Street.

Top: The spire of Trinity Church, later the base for a sundial at the Infirmary, now at the Countess of Chester Hospital.
Bottom: Replica Victorian postbox outside the Town Hall.

The 'Mayor's Parlour' is now in the Grosvenor Museum.

INCORPORATION

Gentlemen of distinction, after giving an oath to be faithful and true to the King and the Corporation, might be admitted to the King's Arms Kitchen Incorporation, a unique club with its own mock council chamber, mayor, sheriff, recorder, town clerk and aldermen. During meetings several wagers were recorded which usually included the loser buying a round and paying a fee to the winner, for example:

'that Bonaparte dies before the next races
'that no victory is gained by the French in 1800
'that Pitt (chancellor) was born in 1750'

as well as bets on the future prices of items in the market place. When strangers visited they were urged to occupy the Mayor's seat and then told that it was customary for anyone sitting there to buy a round of drinks for all present. The Incorporation was founded about 1770. After their last election in 1897, the mock Mayor's Parlour became just another room in the King's Arms Kitchen pub until it closed in 1979, but the locals made good use of the Mayor's chair as a regular source of free drinks from American soldiers in World War II.

153

Canalware

Looking forward to a new era of trade and wealth for the city, the Mayor cut the first sod of the Chester Canal on 18th May 1772. A twenty-one gun salute was fired and the church bells were rung.

Only eight years later, shares were almost worthless. The original plan was to cut the canal to Middlewich to join into the main network but the canal ended at Nantwich. Trade was slow, bridges collapsing and, by 1787, the canal was virtually unusable.

The ropes linking canal boats and horses have left their mark under the city walls cutting deep into the sandstone bedrock.

Meanwhile the Ellesmere Canal Company were having their own problems. The company's objective was to link the rivers Mersey, Severn and Dee. The first section, which promised to give a quick return for investment, was between Chester and Liverpool (ending at Whitby Wharf - now Ellesmere Port - on the Mersey). Cut by 1795 this Wirral Arm was immediately

The sharp bend created at the junction of the Ellesmere and Chester canals needed an iron hook so that boats could be pulled to the outer corner of the bend before turning.

Snowy, in towing regalia, pulled boats here until 1990. A children's book about her was published the same year.

successful with coal 'flats' and packetboats. However, the original route from the Dee south to Pontcysyllte Aqueduct near Llangollen had to be abandoned. The Chester Canal shareholders, realising that their future profits lay in linking the canals, threatened to stop supplying water to the Wirral Arm unless a link was made at the eastern end of the Chester Canal as well. This link to Nantwich was completed in 1805 to everyone's satisfaction, the same year the Montgomery Canal link reached the Severn. Buoyed by new business, the two companies merged in 1813.

Junctions were made with the Trent and Mersey Canal in 1827 and with the Birmingham and Liverpool Canal in 1835. However, by 1846 the railways played a large part in forward planning and the canal became part of the Shropshire Union Railways and Canal Company, only to be leased to the London and North Western Railways a year later.

1775 Chester Chronicle published.
1776 George Harding 10+ years old marries Jane Darlington a sprightly 84 year old. First flat boat from the Dee to the Chester Canal.
1778 On April 5th a huntsman of the Chester Harriers, for a wager, rides around the walls, leaping two turnstiles, in 9½ minutes.
The Watergate demolished. Thomas Harrison's Folliot House built.
1779 Two Roman hypocausts found.
1782 Joseph Turner builds Bridgegate. 8 metre 'fish' weighing over 4 tons caught at Lower Ferry pulled ashore by 10 horses.
[Montgolfier brothers build first outdoor hot-air balloon (launched April 1783).]

'President'
An early 20th century steam narrowboat from the fleet of Fellows, Moreton & Clayton Ltd.

155

Competition with Great Western Railways in this part of the country kept the canal system viable and the company ran its own boats until 1921 when 'economic conditions' made it 'impossible to continue'. Boats, horses and equipment were sold although the canal was kept open for private traders. The following year the 'Shroppie' became a legal part of L&NWR which, in turn, became part of London, Midland and Scottish Railways. Finally the canals were nationalised. Nowadays the British Waterways (Board), established in 1963, undertakes the upkeep of the canal.

Ropemarks have also cut into the iron of the roving bridge where horses, changing towpaths by following the contorted passage, did not have to be untied from the boats they pulled.

The crane inside
'Telford's Warehouse'
now a popular
canalside pub.

The outside of the
warehouse is shown
on the right of the
sketch overleaf.

TELFORD

Thomas Telford was the General Agent,
Surveyor, Engineer, Architect and
Overlooker of the Works on the Ellesmere
Canal for a salary of £300 per annum
under William Jessop, the Chief Engineer.

However, Telford's proficiency, particularly
with his famous iron aqueduct at Pontcysyllte
near Llangollen, soon had him promoted
into Jessop's position.

Thomas
Telford
1757–
1834

157

CANAL PACKET

Shortly after the Wirral Arm of the canal opened,
a packet boat to Liverpool ran from Chester.
The boat, pulled by two horses, could reach speeds
of 12 miles an hour or so. This meant that
passengers could, for 1s6d – 1st Class or 1s – 2nd Class,
reach Liverpool in three hours, using the Countess
of Bridgewater Steamboat to cross the Mersey
and complete the journey. This smooth, speedy
and interesting trip, compared to coach travel
on bumpy roads, made shopping in Liverpool
all the fashion. As a result, the proprietor
had to take on the Coach & Horses public
house, within the walls, for extra beds.

Left: Copy of an advertisement for the Canal Tavern.
Below: The Canal Tavern and Canal Packet.

The adoption of THE STEAM BOAT, which is on the most improved construction, in preference to the Sailing Packet, gives a decided superiority to this mode of conveyance and ensures the passage in three hours,—frequently in less time.

. The Proprietor will not be accountable for parcels above £2. value,

unless entered and paid for accordingly.

Parcels and Luggage taken in at Mr. Jones's, Bear and Billet, Lower Bridge-street; Mr. Hooley's. Coach-and-Horses; Mr. Thomas's, Pied Bull, Northgate-str.; Mr. Griffith's, Canal Tavern; and at Mr. Hickson's, Tower Wharf.

The time of the Packet leaving Liverpool for Chester will be precisely one hour later than stated in this Table.

The Ellesmere Canal Packet,

WILL SAIL FROM THE TOWER WHARF, CHESTER,

FOR ELLESMERE PORT, WHERE IT MEETS A STEAM PACKET FOR LIVERPOOL, EACH DAY AS FOLLOWS:

JULY.			AUGUST.			SEPTEMBER.		
Days.	H.	M.	Days.	H.	M.	Days.	H.	M.
Tu 1	1	E 0	F 1	2	E 0	M 1	5	M 30
W 2	2	0	S 2	3	0	Tu 2	6	30
Th 3	4	M 0 & 2 30 E	Su 3	5	M 30	W 3	7	0*
F 4	5	0 & 3 0	M 4	6	30	Th 4	8	0*
S 5	5	30 & 3 0	Tu 5	7	0*	F 5	9	0*
Su 6	7	0 & 4 0	W 6	8	0*	S 6	9	30
M 7	7	0*	Tu 7	9	0*	Su 7	10	0*
Tu 8	8	0*	F 8	10	0*	M 8	11	0*
W 9	9	0*	S 9	11	0*	Tu 9	11	30*
Th 10	9	30*	Su 10	11	0*	W 10	12	0
F 11	10	0*	M 11	12	0*	Th 11	1	E 0
S 12	11	0*	Tu 12	12	0*	F 12	2	0
Su 13	12	0*	W 13	1	E 0	S 13	2	30
M 14	1	E 0	Tu 14	2	0	Su 14	4	M 0 & 3 0 E
Tu 15	2	0	F 15	2	0	M 15	6	0
W 16	2	30	S 16	4	M 30 & 3 0 E	Tu 16	6	30
Th 17	4	M 0 & 3 0 E	Su 17	5	30 & 4 0	W 17	7	0
F 18	5	30 & 3 0	M 18	7	0	Th 18	8	0
S 19	6	30 & 4 0	Tu 19	7	0	F 19	8	0
Su 20	7	0 & 5 0	W 20	8	0	S 20	9	0
M 21	7	30	Th 21	9	0*	Su 21	9	30*
Tu 22	8	0	F 22	9	0*	M 22	10	0*
W 23	9	0	S 23	10	0*	Tu 23	10	0*
Th 24	9	0*	Su 24	10	0*	W 24	11	0*
F 25	10	0*	M 25	11	0*	Th 25	12	0
S 26	10	0*	Tu 26	11	0*	F 26	12	0
Su 27	11	0*	W 27	12	0*	S 27	1	E 0
M 28	11	0*	Th 28	1	E 0	Su 28	2	0
Tu 29	12	0	F 29	1	0	M 29	2	0
W 30	1	E 0	S 30	2	0	Tu 30	5	M 30
Th 31	2	0	Su 31	4	M 30 & 2 30 E			

CHARLES HICKSON, desirous of deserving the patronage he has experienced since his rental of the BOATS between CHESTER and LIVERPOOL, informs the Nobility, and Gentry, and the Public in general, that he has fitted up BATHS for HOT BATHING. in FRESH and SALT WATER, and SHOWER BATHS.---For the accommodation of LADIES, NEW BATHING HOUSES are erected in more convenient situations than heretofore.

The HOUSE at ELLESMERE PORT is neatly fitted for the accommodation of those desirous of having LODGINGS during the BATHING SEASON, and the terms are as moderate as possible.

John Fletcher, printer, Foregate-street, Chester.

Canal Packet timetable 1823   CR 60/4/13

LIBRARY

Chester's first public library opened in White Friars during
1773 with an annual subscription of a guinea (£1/1/-). It moved
to the Commercial Buildings in Northgate Street during
1815 but after the Free Public Libraries Act of 1850 a
library was opened in St John Street in 1877 (now demolished).
The present library site belonged to a coachmaker in 1850
and became the Westminster Works of J.A. Lawson & Co.
Coach Builders, Harness Makers and Motor Engineers in
1902. The company had ceased trading here by 1914.
After a variety of uses it was converted into the
Library building, retaining the terracotta frontage,
and opened in October 1984.

*The First Duke of
Westminster.
(1825-99)*

The Library

AERONAUTS

The Montgolfier brothers (paper makers) launched the first outdoor hot-air balloon, made of paper, on 25th April 1783 and in June 1783 their paper-lined, hot-air balloon rose into the air 1830 metres, opening the floodgates to a host of experimenters and balloonists. Professor Charles of the Acadamie Francaise, thinking that the brothers had used the new 'light-air' gas, unknowingly made history with the first hydrogen balloon in August the same year. The brothers launched a duck, rooster and sheep in front of Louis XVI and Marie Antoinette during October. On 21st November, de Rozier and the Marquis d'Arlandes made the first human free flight. Others heard the news and used their own balloons. One wonders whether de Rozier had grasped the difference between 'light-air' and hot-air. On his last fateful flight in June 1785 he appears to have ignited a naked flame at 600 metres under his hydrogen balloon, with explosive results!

Three men with interests in flying came to Chester Castle during 1785. The Italian, Vincenzo Lunardi, had made a British flight in London during September 1784. It was believed, at the time, to be the first British flight. It certainly received the most publicity, resulting in countrywide acclaim for Lunardi, who followed it up with a tour to other British cities, living off the profits and gifts that his public acclaim gave him.

The Chester Chronicle of Friday 12th August 1785 states, 'Tuesday last about four o'clock Mr Lunardi made a second aerial voyage from the New Fort Liverpool; he descended at Tiverton... on Wednesday evening he arrived at the White-Lion in this city; where numbers immediately flocked to see this intrepid aeronaut, whose affability cannot fail of procuring the esteem as his courage does the admiration and confidence of Englishmen.'

1784 The Grosvenors spend £15,000 in 90 alehouses to ensure election to Parliament.

1785 Wishing steps built. Lt French flies Lunardi's balloon from the castle to Macclesfield. Six days later Mr Baldwin flies to Risley Moss near Warrington.

1788 Thomas Harrison builds the new Chester Castle. The usual punishment of the period is meted out at Chester Assizes: Isaac Sidebotham and Rebecca Heathcote, the former for stealing a cow and the latter for stealing a quantity of wearing apparel, received sentence of death.

1790 Green Cap day school begins. (Closed 1901).

On Friday 26th August, Lunardi apologised 'for the accident which delayed the ascent of his balloon to so late an hour': he had finally taken off on the Monday before and flown to Hatton Heath, six miles distant.

On Wednesday 31st August, Lieutenant George French rose three yards in Lunardi's second balloon then touched down again. French threw out his ballast along with his provisions and even his hat and coat, whereupon he flew 31 miles to Butler's Mills.

On Friday 2nd September the newspaper informed the public that, 'Mr Lunardi present[s] his respectful compliments to the public with thanks for the favours that he has already received and begs leave to inform them that he has resigned his place in his balloon to T.B.Esq a Gentleman of Chester.'

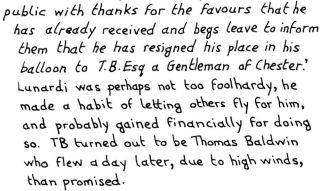

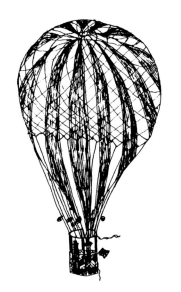

Lunardi was perhaps not too foolhardy, he made a habit of letting others fly for him, and probably gained financially for doing so. TB turned out to be Thomas Baldwin who flew a day later, due to high winds, than promised.

Baldwin was a native of Chester, born in 1742. He resigned as a Huntingdon curate in 1783 and tried to reach the heavens in a different manner. He experimented with balloons and even submitted a design for a grand naval air balloon in 1784 but this was never developed.

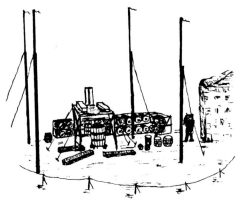

Perhaps with mixed emotions, he then hired Lunardi's balloon, after first launching a small display model of his own. In 1786 his own story of the flight was published.

Lunardi's balloon was inflated with hydrogen made from iron filings and sulphuric acid.

AIROPAIDIA:
CONTAINING
THE NARRATIVE OF A
BALLOON EXCURSION
from CHESTER, the eighth of September, 1785,
taken from MINUTES made DURING the voyage

' On Thursday the 8th of September 1785, at IX in the Morning was first fired one of the Cannons (a six pounder) from the Castle-yard to inform the City and Neighbourhood that the necessary Preparations were making to inflate the Balloon...

'At X o'Clock the process began with the Inflation of an airistatic Globe eighteen Feet in Circumference of Silk Tiffany made the latter End of the Year 1783 and decorated with Painting, Mottoes and Devices: in the Performance of which little Work, Mr Baldwin was the Sole Projector, Architect, Workman and Chymst... It was intended to serve as a sort of Pioneer, to deleneate the Track of the great Balloon. It fell at some Miles Distant, tis said unfortunately on a Hedge and was presently torn to Pieces by the Eagerness and Avarice of the Pursuers, who expected and undeservedly obtained the Reward promised in the Letter appended to it. '

_____

As well as a barometer, thermometer and compass, the balloon carried, ' Down or feathers - to be loose in the Pocket and thrown out when entwined in Clouds or at any other Time to see the Rise or Fall of the Balloon.' Also taken were a pocket book with two red lead pencils (pointed both ends), a pointed knife, a bottle of brandy and water (for experiments), a cork screw, confectionaries such as bread, biscuits and fruit, 2 needles with large eyes - raw silk already threaded and knotted, a map on a board - also to serve as a table, dutch twine, 3 flags, a yard of thin ribbon, a magnet and iron filings

Bewick
Woodcut

163

in a pewter dish and cover, eight bladders - half blown and different colours for decoration, a speaking trumpet and a live pigeon, not forgetting 'Pepper, Salt, Ginger to try the Effects of Tastes which have been said to become insipid on the Peak of Teneriffe'.

At first the breeze carried the anxious aeronaut in the wrong direction, - toward the sea — but then it turned northwest and he flew over Hoole and Trafford. 'The Pepper, Salt and Ginger were tasted, and found to retain their Pungency: contrary to what Travellers have reported from the Peak of Teneriffe'. After several miles the balloon started to descend and when 'approaching a third hedge the Aironaut cut away the Barometer-Frame; threw out the basket with the Bottle and Tunning Dish; the Speaking Trumpet; the Woollen Glove; the remaining half Mile of Twine in the Reel with the result that the Car cleared the Hedge', only to land at Kingsley. He took off again and proceeded to Rixton (Risley) Moss near Warrington.

After his book, containing the first aerial views, was published in 1796, little is known of Baldwin. He had inherited Hoole Hall in 1793 and died in 1804.

Not only the R101 airship, but also the spire of Holy Trinity Church, Chester in 1929.

wishing steps

Run up and down these steps, built in 1785, without drawing a breath and your wish may come true. The steps were once said to answer maidens' wishes for a husband but the tale has grown with the telling.

The wishing steps at the southern corner of the city walls.

1792 Steam mill recorded in Steam Lane (now Steam Mill Street). For a wager a boy runs twice around the walls in 23 minutes. The same year a man hops 151 yards in 46 hops at the Roodee after betting he could hop 150 yards in 50 hops.
1793 Bridge of Sighs built over canal.
1797 [First pound notes issued in England.]
1800 Pillory and stocks removed from the Cross. Leadshot tower built.
1801 The 'drop' first used in executions at Northgate Gaol. Population 15,052. Union flag hoisted at the castle.
1802 Mayor holds first court at the Exchange.
1803 Bull-baiting at the Cross forbidden. Pentice demolished.

The Propylaeum, engraving published 1817.

Propylaeum

During the late 18th century the outer bailey of the medieval Chester Castle was completely transformed into 'one of the most powerful monuments of the Greek Revival in the whole of England'. As well as the Propylaeum (pillared entrance), the courthouse and the Panopticon (county gaol now replaced by County Hall) were planned by architect Thomas Harrison, a Yorkshire carpenter's son who had studied in Italy and was impressed by the 'magnificence of the ages.'

As part payment for his services, Harrison was given a piece of land opposite where he built St Martin's Lodge overlooking the Roodee and, in the distance, the Jubilee Tower on Moel Famau which he designed. Here this 'modest' man, 'shy, reserved and abrupt in his manner' but 'clear and ready in explaining with his pencil', died in 1829 at the age of 84, leaving the city with a wealth of buildings for the future.

Thomas Harrison 1744-1829

The Bridge of Sighs by
the Northgate.

BRIDGE OF SIGHS

1808 Northgate Gaol closed; prisoners moved to new House of Correction. Commercial newsroom built. A Xmas pie given by Earl Grosvenor for the Exchange banquet weighs 69 kilos.

1809 Over 70 ale houses within the walls.

1810 Chester United Gas Co. opens in Cuppin Street.

1813 New clock on St Peter's Church.

1814 9th May "CURIOUS CASE - On opening one of the graves in St Peter's Church, in Chester, last week, the body of a young woman, which had been buried upwards of 80 years, was found quite perfect: her long auburn tresses, and placid countenance, presented a most interesting spectacle."

The small bridge, complete with iron railings, was built in 1793 by Joseph Turner for £10. Prisoners from the Northgate Gaol (now demolished) used it for access to the chapel and the 'apartment made for prisoners' in the Bluecoat Hospital. It became known as the Bridge of Sighs (or Bridge of Death) after it was used by those condemned to die who, after their final visit to the chapel, crossed back to the gaol for 'the drop'. In 1821 the City Assembly ordered that the redundant bridge be removed but this was never done although the iron railings were later removed for conversion into munitions.

Madonna
and Child
by
Johann
Burgman
after
Lucas
Cronach I.

CATERPILLARS' NET

At Chester Cathedral a small picture is on an unusual art medium. Austrian Tyrole Innsbruck painter Johann Burgman (d1825) painted this picture on a caterpillars' net. It is a copy of Maria Hilf Madonna by Lucas Cronach I which has been, since 1630, at St Jakob's Church, Innsbruck.

The small gregarious ermine moth 'Hyponomeuta Evonymella', which can be found in Britain and on the Continent, is the size of a clothes moth. It builds a large net or sack attached to branches of bird cherry to protect its caterpillars who go out to strip the leaves off the plant then return for protection.

The oldest remaining leadshot tower in Britain.

LEADSHOT

Chester has been a port for the export of lead from North Wales since Roman times, with over 4,000 tons passing through in the 1760s and 70s. This made the canalside site ideal for Walkers, Parker &Co to build a new lead works at the end of the 18th century. In 1783 William Watts of Bristol had patented his:

> 'process for making smallshot perfectly globular in form and without dimples, notches and imperfections which other shot hereto manufactured usually have on their surface.'

As early as the 17th century British troops were issued with casks of lead shot for their muskets, but much of it suffered from pockmarks on the surface, making it inefficient and even dangerous. The 51 metre high leadshot tower, built in 1800, supplied ammunition for the British forces in France who finally overcame Napolean at Waterloo.

Shot was produced by dropping molten lead, containing arsenic, through a sort of collander, into a wooden tank of water at the foot of the tower. The process was automated in 1946. The tower originally had sandstone steps which were removed in the early 20th century and replaced with an iron ladder which lasted until 1968 when a new staircase was built. The present external lift was added in 1971.

The works beside the tower dealt with other lead products. By 1812 a rolling mill and piping machine had been built and the works continued to expand, transportation in the mid-19th century being assured by the railway built along the northern edge of the site. Leadshot of 8mm diameter was needed to add into molten steel for the lead alloy process. This was produced by dropping lead through a fine 'card' for 7 metres into a dry hopper. In the 1960s, machine shot was introduced but by the 1980s tower shot was still commercially viable over machine-made shot, and so production continued.

Michael Hoddinott records an unusual tale in his manuscript history of the Lead Works (available at Chester Record Office): on one evening in the winter of 1988/9, after the works had shut, the security man and his daughter both saw an old lady with a long, heavy bag near the paint building. On following the figure through the yard, the guard could not find any trace of her. Later, when he mentioned this to some of the older workers, they recognised the description of Mrs Cox who had worked in the shot department. She had left the company long before the guard was employed. Each day she brought cigarettes for the men in a long bag, using the route described by the security man, through the shot works.

1817 Gas laid to houses. George Batenham produces etchings of the main streets.
1819 Gas lights introduced on the city streets.
1820 Watergate House built. Ladies regularly use sedan chairs.
1821 Lamb Row fell into the street. Population of combined parishes: about 20,000.
1823 [Death penalty abolished for many crimes in England.]
1824 First Tradesman's Cup (since 1893 called Chester Cup) run with six horses. Mr Sadler flew a gas balloon from the castle to Utkinton and Tarporley.
1826 City of Chester Waterworks incorporated.

Of bonfires & gunpowder

1564 Thomas Yeaton for gounepowder at the triumthe
                 by Maister Mayres appoyntment   xiii^s

1567 From the Dean of Chapters Treasurer's Accounts:

          Pd for the bonfyer at Midsummer xxiij^s viij^d
          & to Browen for making the bonfyre   iiij^d
  Item paid for a brode clothe against the Whitson pleas   vj^s vij^d
 Item for a barrell of bere to geve to the pleares to make them to drink vi^s
    Item for packe threed at Witson Daye   ij^d
  Item for gorses on MidSomer even to the Bonfyre   vj^d

1709 Fire regulations:

… no person shall have or keep any more or greater quantity than two pounds
of Gunpowder at any one tyme in any shop sellar or lower room within
this city except such gunpowder and shall be kept in any carrierss
warehouse or shall be brought into this city to be exported into Ireland
not being kept more than forty eight hours in such Carriers Warehouse…

1761 *Exerpt from Improvement Act:* …in case any Person or Persons shall throw, disperse, or set Fire to any Squibs, Rockets, Serpents, Crackers, or other Fire Works, or shall fire off any Gun or Pistol, expend and set Fire to, or cause to be fired, any Gunpowder alone, or with any other Ingredient, or shall make or assist at the making of any openfire, usually called Bonfires or shall throw, disperse, or carry about any openfire, in any of the Streets, Lanes, Rows, Passages, or other Places within the said City… for every such seperate Offence the Sum of Ten Shillings, to be levied…

1764 Order from the Precedent's Book 21st September:
Constables on the 22nd September are 'to walk Rounds from 5 o'Clock to 10 o'Clock in the Evening that you apprehend and take up all persons whatsoever that should throw, Cast or fire any Squibs or Fireworks in any Street House Row or Passage'

1772 On 5th November Chester suffered its own gunpowder plot, except there was no Guy Fawkes and no plot. A puppet show was taking place in Eatons' Rooms, just off Watergate Street. A large audience had assembled and 'the puppets were going through their strange evolutions, when, by some appalling misfortune, eight hundredweight of gunpowder lodged in a warehouse below suddenly blew up with a tremendous report, killing the showman and twenty-two others, eighty-three besides being more or less injured'.

1805 Poster
CR 632/1

GLORIOUS
NAVAL VICTORIES.
Twenty-Four Sail of the Line,
BELONGING TO THE
FRENCH AND SPANIARDS,
TAKEN AND DESTROYED BY THE
English Fleet.

THE INHABITANTS of the City of CHESTER, are requested during the ILLUMINATION on this GLORIOUS EVENT, not to make, sell, give, or let off any Squibs, Rockets, Serpents, Crackers or other Fire-works, or to fire off any Gun, Pistol or Gun-powder, or make any Bonfire; Offences which are subject to several Penalties by Acts of Parliament, and which it may be recollected occasioned *a very melancholy accident in this City, some Years ago:*

THE MAYOR, AND OTHER MAGISTRATES

GIVE NOTICE, That all Persons Committing any of the above Offences, will be Prosecuted, and the Penalties rigorously enforced; and that Constables and others, will be stationed in different parts of the City to give informations of such offenders.

Exchange, Wednesday Morning,
20th. November. 1805.

Taking the biscuit

As late as 1868, apprentices in this area, as well as signing an indenture or contract, also had a biscuit broken over their head. Another biscuit, inscribed with the date, master's name and apprentice's name was then given to the newly bound youth. One, given to a bookbinder's apprentice when he was fifteen reads 'Thomas Clarke, January 8th, 1921, to Edward Pover, Bookbinder.' His indenture shows that he was 'inrolled in the Pentice office of the City of Chester' on the 8th February that year. Thomas Clarke became a freeman in 1831.

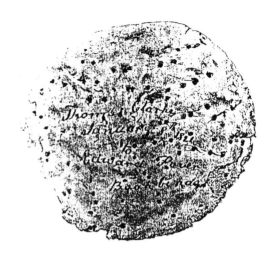

Thomas Clarke's binding biscuit.

Richard Bolland had his own apprentice or binding biscuit given to him in 1821. He completed his time 'truly and faithfully' and became a Freeman of the city. His company in Eastgate Street went on to make cakes for at least seven royal weddings.

LIONS

A stone carving of a British lion standing victorious over a French eagle was made in 1815 for Palmer's exhibition in Pall Mall. It bore the motto Animo non Astuta (by courage not cunning) and referred to the victory over Napoleon. It stood, after the exhibition, at Folliot House in Northgate Street until a landlord of the Pied Bull took it to the Grosvenor Arms at Pulford but now the Pulford pub has two new lions.

The former Lion Brewery in Pepper Street was founded in 1642. Under it was a tunnel used to sally the besiegers in the Civil War. The brewhouse was rebuilt in 1875 for Bents Brewery. Bents' lion was saved by Mr D J Tomlinson of the Chester Civic Trust when the brewery was demolished, and eventually remounted on top of the lift shaft of the new car park.

High tides create a bore (a wave) which runs upriver hitting anything in the way.

Grosvenor Bridge

Thomas Harrison first submitted plans for the proposed new bridge in 1818. In Lancaster he had designed Skerton Bridge over the Lune, which was copied by John Rennie for the Waterloo and London bridges. James Trubshaw (1777-1853) said that he was, 'convinced the arch will be the largest and finest stone arch in Europe and will consequently be a lasting monument to the glory and superiority of Great Britain'.

Enormous stones 1.68 metres x 46cm x 46cm were cut for the Grosvenor Bridge.

Harrison was paid nearly £400 for his work and plans but died before work was started in 1827. The (then) largest single span sandstone arch in the world crosses nearly 70 metres with a rise of nearly 13 metres and cost £49,824 excluding toll houses, gates, the new road and other works. When the final arch stone was placed, the structure dropped a mere 67mm.

On Wednesday 17th October 1832, Princess Victoria and the Duchess of Kent were driven through the triumphal arch mounted in the centre of the bridge, decorated with the royal arms and a crown. A 21 gun salute was fired and, when the carriage of the royal visitors reached the arch, the royal standard was raised. The future queen gave a short speech naming the bridge.

Trubshaw's model of Thomas Harrison's Grosvenor Bridge was packed and brought to Chester by mail coach. It was exhibited in the Grand Jury Room (also built by Harrison) of the castle. Later it was put in the Water Tower Gardens and, in 1979, restored and set in its present position in Castle Drive.

Silhouette

Before the invention of the camera, other means were used.

c1828 Browns of Chester trading.

1829 Cheshire County Lunatic Asylum opened.

1830 Exchequer Court abolished. Morgan's Mount railed.

1831 Population 21,363

1832 Princess Victoria opens Grosvenor Bridge: 1st toll.

1833 Billy 'Obbies Field on map of Groves.

1835 Only one sheriff from this year after Council of the Borough of Chester set up under the Municipal Corporations Act. Ratepayers elect councillors.

1836 Tolls at city gates discontinued. Mayor refuses to pay for Chester hand so clerk gives it away.

1838 Foundation stone of the Chester & Crewe Railway.

1840 Chester College opens. Steam engine 'Wirral' pulls 10 carriages into Chester.

1841 First steam boat on Dee above the weir.

1843 Roodee Cross moved (beside walls for 10 years).

1845 Chester & Holyhead Railway begun by felling trees near the Water Tower.

1846 Roodee railway bridge built. (It collapsed under a train in 1847.) Tidal Harbours Commission criticise River Dee Company for overriding interest in land sales. Chester College moves to W.E. Gladstone building.

CR 655/7

An advertisement from the Chester Chronicle 25th August 1826

EDWARD HALL,

Commonly called TEDDY HALL, a well known character of this city.

THE above likeness is taken from the original, which may be seen at the Artists (from London) No. 51, Bridge-street Row, where for a very short time (in consequence of being under previous engagements) they are taking LIKENESSES warranted exact, (by a machine on a Mathematical principle, which is certain of correctness) with frame and glass included, for ONE SHILLING only. Likewise, superior SHADED PORTRAITS, at TWO SHILLINGS and SIX-PENCE, &c. with frame and glass included.

The Artists have regularly studied at the Royal Academy of Arts, British Museum, and most of the principal Galleries in London.

They likewise, beg to inform the inhabitants of Chester, that since leaving London, they have visited Sheffield, Hull, York, and Liverpool, where one of them at present remains, but will soon be at Chester, and at each of the above places, met with every encouragement, particularly from the higher class, many of whose likenesses, and of the nobilities throughout Yorkshire, they have been permitted to retain as specimens; they therefore hope, that the respectability of their situation will induce those Ladies and gentlemen to honor them with a visit who otherwise would not.

The Artists will attend from 10 o'clock in the morning till 8 in the evening.

Camera obscura

In 1838 the Mechanics Institute installed a camera obscura in Bonewaldesthorne Tower. A convex lens projected images of outside objects onto a round white table or screen within the darkened upper room. Roberts Chester Guide of 1851 told of the camera 'which is situated on the upper part of the tower, and is well worthy of notice. We can promise the reader very great gratification and amusement from this excellent instrument which will furnish him with a most charming prospect of the diversified and lovely scenery which nature has so profusely spread around. The beautiful view of the winding Dee and the picturesque country on its banks is most delightful, and cannot fail to excite very pleasurable emotions.' The original obscura fell into disuse and the optics were lost.

In 1984 Peter Drew of Bedford Astronomical Supplies, who had made an obscura at Greenwich, provided one to the Garden Festival at Stoke-on-Trent. It was resited at Chester. Having had the altitude set manually, its electric motor turns the 150mm lens with a focal length of nearly six metres in a circle over 13 minutes to display views of the wall and canal.

The camera obscura on top of Bonewaldesthorne Tower. At present the city council have closed the tower to the public.

1847 Chester General Station opens.
1849 Architectural, Archaeological and Historic Society of Chester founded. Public swimming and shower baths open near Water Tower.
1850 400,000 passengers through Chester General Station. 'London Bridge' over Feathers Lane. Public baths taken over by city. Average 300 dozen clothes washes each month and 300 swims each month.
1851 Population 27,616. Cabs from station to city 1 shilling.
1852 First Queen's Park Suspension Bridge built.
1853 Firemen/police resign, as work is too onerous. TSB building erected. Chester-Australia last voyage.

STATION CLOCK

The steam train 'Wirral' and ten carriages arrived in Chester on the line from Birkenhead during 1840, the same year the Chester & Crewe Railway opened. Other lines followed and all were served by a temporary station until the city's General Station opened in 1848. The contractor (whose bust can now be found in the Cathedral) Thomas Brassey built it to a design by Francis Thompson (the architect for Derby Station) and C H Wild.

Chester General Station: 19th century engraving showing the original clock position.

Sets of towers on the 307 metre long Italianate frontage took away the long straight lines whilst incorporating the buildings into a whole without emphasising a central point, except for a central clock. Local time was used in Britain until Railway Time had to be used for timetables. Greenwich Mean Time was adopted in 1880.

By 1850 there were six railway companies operating in Chester Station. There were seven miles of line, 18 cranes and 51 turntables there. With 40 goods trains a day, over 380,000 tonnes were handled that year with 400,000 passengers passing through the doors.

Chester General Station with the off-centre clock.

A 19th century guide book suggests that: 'If after your late journey, you feel any of the cravings of the inner man, — if dinner a-la-mode lie uppermost in your thoughts — if you would enjoy an invigorating cup of coffee, unimpeachable pastry, a good glass of ale, or a fragrant cigar, take a turn in the REFRESHMENT ROOMS, and the utmost wish of your soul will be incontinently gratified'

Afterwards, a horsedrawn cab to any part of the city was a shilling.

With trade brisk, a new approach road was needed. City Road was built to the station and opened, in 1866, through a temporary triumphal arch emblazoned with the arms of the city and the railway companies. However, incoming passengers needed to be assured of the time, so the timepiece was moved.

The station clock viewed up City Road

MUSIC HALL

The Chapel of St Nicholas was built in 1280 as a guild chapel, but by 1488 the chapel was rededicated to St Oswald to replace the parish church which had been inside St Werburgh's – a part of this former Saxon minster had always been used for parishioners: during the 13th century they probably held services in the south aisle of the nave. By 1539 parishioners had regained St Oswald's within the south transept of the monastery church. (The parish church was later (1828-30) partitioned from the cathedral and then the parishioners moved to the new St Thomas of Canterbury Church in Parkgate Road.)

The Chapel of St Nicholas fell into disuse. After the surrender of the abbey it was, for a short time, used as the new King's School.

In 1545, the citizens purchased the building to be used as the new Common Hall using the profits from a 'common bargayne' of 52 tons of iron, being 3 tons worth £24 given by the Mayor and 'Sences Dermiche hyspanyard.' In 1547 it was decreed that 'no maner [of] person inhabyting the said citie shall from hensforth by no maner of wares or merchandises that shall coum to this cytye to be soulde in grosse befor the same be brought and layde doune in the comon haule of this cytie...'
This decree, that all wholesale goods must be sold at the Common Hall, included a list of fees for selling them including:
   'that every person bringing any nales or hardware to this citie to be soulde shall bringe the same to the said comen haule and pay for every pak waying two hundryth wight & above   1ᵈ
   'that every Kendall man comyng to this citie with eny clothe or other merchandies... pay for every pak 1ᵈ
   'that every man shall pay for every doussyn calfe skins that is soulde   1ᵈ '

In 1567 it was decreed that no one should receive any goods into their 'houses, cellers, sollers or lofts' to be sold 'in grosse'.

The Music Hall in St Werburgh Street is now a shop, its 3 metre extension was built in 1854.

The lower room 'was appointed for the storage of wool, corn, cloth and other commodities to be vended and sold by Forreiners and Strangers, at times allowable in the city,' the upper rooms for '... the Assemblies, Elections, Courts'. Daniel King in 1651 states: 'Not far from the Pendice, towards the Abby Gate, is the Common-Hall of the City. Which is a very great House of Stone: and serveth instead of their Guild-Hall or Town House'

In 1695 the new 'Exchange' including council offices was built in the present Town Hall square. The old chapel became the Wool Hall. In 1727 it became a play house and was upgraded to the Theatre Royal in 1773. In 1854 the building was extended by 3 metres and became the new Music Hall. The new frontage was designed by James Harrison. During 1867 Charles Dickens read 'Marigold' and 'Trial' here. In a letter he wrote that, 'the hall is like a Methodist Chapel in low spirits, and with a cold in its head.' In another he reported, 'At Chester we read in a snowstorm and a fall of ice. I think it was the worst weather I ever saw. Nevertheless the people were enthusiastic.'

In 1921 the Music Hall became the oldest building in the world to be used as a cinema. The Music Hall Cinema showed Al Jolson in the first 'Talkie' during 1927. It closed in 1961 and became the first supermarket within the city walls: Liptons. Since then it has been a shop for Fosters, Reject and Superdrug, but still bears the outlines of its original use.

1854 Bluecoat School enlarged. Blue boy added. King Charles' Tower is an observatory.
1855 Theatre Royal becomes Music Hall.
1858 Crypt buildings built in High Gothic.
1861 King's Arms Kitchen rebuilt.
1862 The Exchange burns down. A new public market founded.
1863 City of Chester Voluntary Fire Brigade formed with 2 steamers, a manual and a horse-drawn tender. Any member swearing fined 5s. Feathers Hotel demolished. Market opens.
1864 Northgate Brewery Co. trades.
1866 City Road built. Last public hanging. Cheshire cattle plague.

Blocked-up Early English archway on the side of St Nicholas' Chapel (the Music Hall).

GREAT EASTERN

Mr William Haswell, master mason, and Mr Musgrave, timberyard owner, were so stirred by the launch of the Great Eastern in 1858 that they carved its length and an anchor into the city wall. They had reason to be impressed. The enormous ship, built in four years by Isambard Kingdom Brunel, had a tonnage of 18,914 tons compared with the average ship which had a tonnage of only a third of that. Designed to carry 4,000 passengers or 10,000 troops, it had the world's first cellular double hull (now recommended for all oil carrying vessels) and the first steering engine. An oscillating engine drove a propeller and two paddles to complement the ship's sails. However, the ship suffered an explosion off Hastings on its maiden voyage and was later used on the transatlantic run to New York, not the Pacific as intended. Later, the ship was used to lay transatlantic cable. In 1874 a ship designed for the purpose made her obsolete and she ended her life as a floating advert for Lewis of Liverpool, lying at anchor with music hall shows and circus acts on board, before being broken up, in 1889, at Tranmere.

Above: The inscription by the kaleyard gate Slope on the wall.

The Great Eastern (built as 'The Leviathan') under repairs on the Cheshire Shore of the Mersey.

Equestrian
Statue by
the Castle.

Riding out

Successful soldiers normally ride home for a hero's welcome but the equestrian statue of Field Marshal Viscount Combermere GCB (1773-1865) shows him heading out. As the Field Marshal was not in the Cheshire Regiment housed nearby, it was not thought fitting that the bronze on granite statue should face the city.

Sir Stapleton Cotton, sixth baronet, first Viscount Combermere, field marshal (1855) colonel 1st life guards (1829) and constable of the Tower of London (1852) was not even born in Chester. As the fifth child of Sir Robert Salusbury Cotton he had his birth at the family seat of Llewenny Hall, Denbighshire. Once in the army, his officer training took him up through the echelons; Wellington declaring that his orders to Stapleton Cotton were carried out with discretion and zeal. As a general by 1825 he served as governor general in India. He sat for the sculpture by Baron Marochetti in the last years of his life. Viscount Combermere was the provincial grand master of the Freemasons in Cheshire.

TUPPENNY MARQUIS

The citizens of Chester, by public subscription, set up a statue by Thorneycroft in the Grosvenor Park at a cost of £3,500 to thank Richard, second Marquis of Westminster, for the park he gave in 1867. The Marquis wears the robes of the Order of the Garter. The original inscription on the white Sicilian marble statue (originally thought to be one piece but later found to have a piece cut in the shoulder), the tallest in England, read '2nd Marquis' and was quickly changed when the similarity between 2d (2 pence) and 2nd led to him being nicknamed the tuppenny marquis.

Billy Hobby's Well

The well in 'Billy 'Obbies field', now at the foot of Grosvenor Park, was used as a wishing well but only, apparently, by girls.

> I lov'd the tales that idle maids would tell,
> Of wonders wrought at Billy Hobby's Well;
> Where love-sick girls with leg immured would stand,
> The right leg 'twas – the other on dry land,
> With face so simple - stocking in the hand –
> Wishing for husbands half a winter's day
> With ninety times the zeal they used to pray

John Douglas designed the stonework around the well in Grosvenor Park

King Charles I

FORESHORTENED

Over 350 years ago, with his last words, "I go from a corruptible to an incorruptible crown where no disturbance can be," King Charles I was executed for treason at the Banqueting House in Whitehall, London. His death warrant had been signed by Oliver Cromwell and 58 others. The king wore two shirts 'lest his shivering be taken as a sign of fear.'

The elaborate mock-17th century design was built in 1882 at 61 Bridge Street Row for Sherrat, David & Co, art dealers. However when the statue turned up it was too tall. A drastic solution, and one that left his head on his shoulders, was needed so the carpenters chopped out a bit of his legs instead.

TRAMS

The Chester Tramways Company, formed in 1878 laid standard gauge rails from Chester Station via Foregate Street to Curzon Street in Saltney. On 21st June 1879 the new tramway opened. Its one-horse cars, far safer on rails than coaches, were painted crimson-lake and cream, the horse having a bell on its collar to warn pedestrians. At first, the driver, paid three shillings a day, was also the conductor but successful operation led to boys being employed to sell tickets and load parcels at a shilling a day.

Shortly after the turn of the century a dozen open-top electric trams, seating 20 upstairs and 23 down, took to the rails, now narrowed to just over a metre. Chester Corporation Tramways were green and cream with a single light at each end. Five new cars were added in 1906. The two and a half mile track was mostly inset with granite setts which extended half a metre each side. The gradient was no more than 1 in 30.

Chester's trams ceased in 1930; to be replaced by ten single and five double-decker buses.

Top: Tramway cable brackets can still be seen on the walls of some Eastgate Street buildings. One has been put to another use, holding the Grosvenor Hotel sign stable in high winds.

Bottom: The present bus depot (opposite Chester General Station) was the original site for the horse tramway sheds. Rails can still be seen there.

Electric trams ran from 1903 until 1930 along Eastgate and Foregate streets.

Chewing gum girl

On the south side of the River Dee, in Overleigh Cemetery lies the gravestone of Mabel Francis Ireland-Blackburn. Although she died of whooping cough she is known locally as the chewing gum (or bubble gum) girl because of a little ditty that is said to have been posted up near the grave to discourage children from chewing and swallowing gum.

> Chewing gum – chewing gum – made of wax
> Brought me to my grave at last.
> When I die, God will say,
> "Throw that dirty stuff away!"

Chewing gum was invented by 1850, when the Chicago Daily Democrat called it a 'new and superior preparation of Spruce Gum'. The origin of the poem was a skipping song. Hundreds of thousands of black and white spots on the Chester streets and rows testify to the fact that gum is regularly thrown away – after use!

'Hush she sleeps' Mabel Francis Ireland-Blackburn (7/4/1866 – 13/11/1869).

...had so many children...

'The death took place on Monday of Mrs Mary Jonas, who earned the proud position among the matrons of England of being the mother of thirty-three children. On no fewer than fifteen occasions she gave birth to twins. This distinction was more than local, for some years ago when "Tit-Bits" offered a copy of that paper for life to the lady who showed a 'record' for contributing to the population of the empire, Mrs Jonas was singled out as the lucky competitor for the prize. Mrs Jonas carried on the business of a furniture dealer in Foregate-street for many years, but latterly had lived with her daughter, Mrs Barnett, Queen Street where she passed away at the good age of 87.'

CHESTER CHRONICLE 9/12/1899

Mrs Mary Jonas' gravestone states that she was 85.
All her sets of twins were a boy and a girl.

Politicians

Benjamin Disraeli (the first earl of Beaconsfield) was elected to Parliament in 1837. By 1868 his imperialist 'Tory' policies, speeches and wit had made him Prime Minister and a friend of Queen Victoria.

He was defeated by William Ewart Gladstone who had entered Parliament as a Conservative but later became a Liberal ('Whig').

Gladstone stood for 'Peace, Retrenchment and Reform', and held power from 1868-74 as well as 1880-85, 1886 and 1892-94.

Gladstone (right) and Disraeli.   Punch 1872

1867 Second Marquis of Westminster gives Grosvenor Park to the city. Charles Dickens gives reading at the Music Hall.

1869 The Town Hall opened on the 15th October by the Prince of Wales (Edward VII). Drill Hall built.

1870 W. Hewitt runs first public omnibus with 2 horses. Roodee Railway Bridge rebuilt.

1871 Chester Natural History Society founded. Amy Dutton in her book disguises Chester as Norminster and refers to eight public houses in Abbot's (Princes) Street. [F.A. Cup started.]

1872 Blue Girls' school opens in Vicars Lane to teach girls to read, understand church, sew, knit and spin.

Living at nearby Hawarden, his hobbies included felling trees with an axe and dissuading the 'ladies of the night'. His anti-imperialist policies were unsuccessful in getting Home Rule for Ireland and his failure to save General Gordon in Khartoum was his undoing. However, he brought about the Secret Ballot in 1872. He opened the country's first teacher training college in Chester during 1842; a conference centre there and three local streets are named after him.

Opposite: Carved heads on the south wing of Chester Cathedral show Disraeli with a sword, Gladstone with a pen.

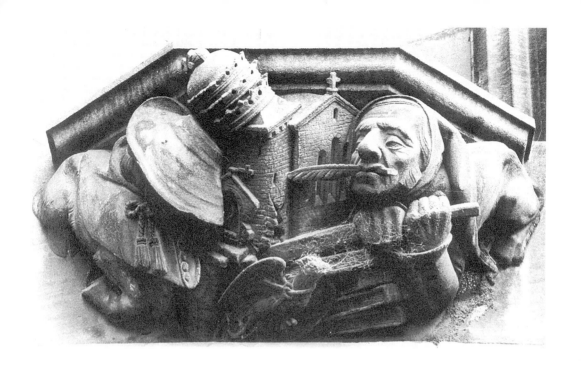

195

Tokens

John Roberts
Ironmonger
HIS PENNY
1669
IN CHESTER

'I promise to pay the bearer on demand...' on bank notes was once a promise to pay in gold but this was not a new idea. King Edward I, who started his great castle building from Chester, saved on bullion by issuing leather money. By Tudor times, tokens of lead, tin and leather were common, while the city of Bristol was granted permission to produce copper tokens for use within a ten mile radius. Despite Charles I issuing farthings on his accession, tokens were still prevalant although Cromwell intended to stop the practice.

It is estimated that over 40,000 different tokens were issued in England during the 17th century, mainly between the years 1648-72, by merchants and councils. There were at least 28 in Chester; the Grosvenor Museum holds several 'pennies' and 'halfpennies' issued by traders between the years 1663 and 1670. Although many are from ironmongers, as might be expected, there are also coins from other traders including a linendraper, and a heart-shaped penny from Samuell Heath, a confectioner.

During George III's reign no copper coins were issued from 1775 until 1797, resulting in more trade tokens being issued, especially within the years 1787-97. In nearby Wrexham, the iron-master and entrepreneur John Wilkinson produced copper pennies under licence, making a 40% profit. His coin could be cashed at his works in Bradley, Willey, Snedshill and Bersham, and later at Liverpool and London. On one side of the pennies, his face resembled King George and he was sarcastically referred to as the 'Iron Monarch'.

In 1812 all the silver coin of the realm had disappeared around Birmingham resulting in tokens of leather or even pasteboard to pay workers' wages. Most 19th century tokens were issued between the years 1811 and 1817. The firms then set up their own shops where tokens could be traded and profits recouped by the issuer. An attempt to end this practice was made in an Act of 1817 which guaranteed that local tokens, where presented to the issuer, were to be exchanged for Bank of England notes. Today some Chester residents use the local 'Alternative Trading System' with traders using 'Devas' instead of pounds or euros.

A Chester token issued between 1857-69 by John Frith, proprietor of the Temperance Hotel in Goss Street. It could be used for food, drink or even accommodation.

Cocoa

'Old Nag' thy head for many a year
Brewed mischief with its gin and beer
Henceforward we prefer thy tail
In hopes that Temperance may prevail.

From 'History of St John's Parish'
by Rev. S Cooper Scott.

Temperance in the city came in all shapes and sizes: the Old Nag's Head, 47-49 Foregate Street was a temperance house by 1877. In 1902 it became the Little Nag's Head Cocoa House but had reverted to an inn by 1910.

Another inn, the Falcon, became the Chester Cocoa House between (at least) the years 1882-1900 and was known as the Falcon Cocoa House between (at least) the years 1904-35 then the manageress, Mrs Davies continued trading as the Falcon Café until (at least) 1952. There was also a cocoa house in the Town Hall, one in Brook Street and another by the Railway Station.

A new movement for Gospel Temperance in Britain was promoted by an American, Richard Booth, during 1882. Richard Cadbury, guaranteeing all costs, invited him to speak in Birmingham. John Cadbury, Richard's ailing father who had been leader of a similar movement in Birmingham, also spoke on several occasions. In three weeks of meetings over 50,000 pledges of total abstinence were made and a Gospel

Temperance Mission set up. Richard Cadbury was a lifelong supporter. On 22nd October 1889 he opened a Temperance Institute which became the home of the UK Alliance, the Band of Hope, the Sunday Closing Association, the Church of England Temperance Society, the National Vigilance Association and others. The Institute housed a large number of books. Total abstainers subscribing for five shillings annually had access to the Institute and its library.

The name cocoa derives from the three syllable word 'cacao' used until the 18th century. This came from the Spanish and like the word chocolate was derived from the Mayan 'xocoatl' (choco= foam or bitter, atl = water or bean according to different authorities). The Aztecs, who founded Mexico in 1325, imported 'cacahuitl' for drinking. Hernando Cortez met (and later killed) the Aztec Emperor of Mexico in the early 16th century and found that chocolate, flavoured with honey and vanilla, was Emperor Montezuma's only beverage and that he drank it before visiting his wives, leading to the assumption that it was an aphrodisiac. The Spanish cultivated cacao trees and kept the chocolate recipe a secret until the beginning of the 17th century. A 'chocolate house' was open in the city of London during 1657. By the end of the century chocolate was being sold in London for around £1 a kilo so that 'none but the rich and famous could afford to drink choclatl'.

At the end of the 18th century, Dr Joseph Fry of Bristol used a steam engine to grind cocoa beans. A Dutch pressing machine was designed by Van Heuten to create cocoa butter in 1828 - used by Cadburys in 1866 to produce pure cocoa powder. Frys made the first commercial chocolate bar in 1847. Milk chocolate was brought into production by Nestlé in 1876, and fondant, which melted on the tongue, by Lindt in 1879.

CHESTER COCOA HOUSE COMP.Y [Limited]

At 5 Brook Street the Smithfield Cocoa House ran from 1888 to 1938 before it became 'dining rooms'. Between 1952 and 1956 it was the Smithfield Café. At the time of writing it is a Greek restaurant. Cocoa isn't on the menu; teetotallers can have the bellydancing without the wine.

The Falcon from 'The Building News' 30/4/1886

Falcon

With its medieval cellar (sometimes claimed to be Roman, but extremely unlikely as it was outside the fortress wall) the Falcon has a long history. Archaeological research has shown that it is only half of a medieval townhouse of the early 13th century.

The Grosvenors bought it from Sir George Hope in 1602 to use as a family town house.

1874 Floating baths open on Dee in Groves.
1875 Northgate Railway Station opens.
1876 Post Office built in St John Street.
1877 Free public library opens in St John Street.
1878 Chester Tramways Bill.
1879 Watch Tower by Wishing Steps taken down. Grosvenor Bridge model erected in Water Tower Gardens (now in Castle Drive). Horse-drawn tramway starts.
1881 Roman gravestones found in city walls near Phoenix Tower. St John's northwest tower collapses; noise heard throughout city. St Oswald's parishioners move to St Thomas of Canterbury in Parkgate Road.

During the Civil War, Richard Grosvenor enclosed the first storey row which, he claimed, made the house too small (see page 51). However this was undoubtedly just a ploy for privacy.

From 1778 for a century it was a pub, then the first Duke of Westminster, true to the temperance spirit— or the working class anyway— had it altered by John Douglas and turned into a cocoa house.

By 1957 the café that it had evolved into was closed and the building stayed empty for a year before it was taken over by the wholesale and textile firm, Montgomery Tomlinson. The industrial premises closed in 1971.

The sign of The Falcon.

A restoration scheme saved the collapsing structure and it was reopened as a pub. Inside, the enclosed row front still remains; as does the wattle-and-daub wall filling on display behind see-through panels. This early plaster was made from branches of hazel covered in a mix of lime, clay and horse-dung.

1882 Royalty Theatre opens on City Road.

1883 Floating baths taken over by Corporation. North and South Wales Bank built by John Douglas next to Eastgate.

1884 Chester Cooperative Society founded. Spital graveyard enclosed.

1885 The Earl of Chester's Volunteer Fire Brigade opened with all members under 45 years old. Chester becomes one parliamentary constituency. Toll on bridges cancelled. Coop opens in Black Diamond Street. Grosvenor Museum built.

1887 St Mary-without-the-walls consecrated.

1888 Chester becomes a County Borough.

The Falcon.

Chester Electric Lighting Station.

Power to the people

Built under the auspices of Professor Kennedy, Chester Electric Lighting Station in Crane Street was operating by 1896 with 48 arc lamps in the city streets (see page 81). Incandescent lamps were installed in 1899.

The legendary engineer S E Britton was responsible for the distribution of the electric power, a Direct Current system of 210/420 volts recommended by the world famous physicist, Lord Kelvin.

This was created by generators driven by triple expansion reciprocating steam engines fed by boilers fitted with chain stokers. Electricity was stored in a large tiled battery room.

By 1910 the maximum capacity of the works was realised so that, in 1911,

The Hydro-electric Power Station, used since 1951 as a water pumping station.

Work was started on the Hydro-electric Power Station situated on the site of the Old Dee Mills (beside the bridge) purchased by the Corporation in 1895.

Architect Francis Graves, in the Sunday Times of 4th April 1988, described the Chester Electric Lighting Building as a 'landmark'. However, in 1999, the Lighting Station faced destruction under the Old Port Regeneration Scheme. The plan was to replace it with a mock-1920s port building for use as an office block. Local residents and five local historians (Len Morgan, Michael Hoddinott, Roy Wilding, Tony Bowerman and the author) complained.

Although the Department of the Environment refused to list the building and demolition permission was granted by the council, the developer changed his mind about previous plans and the building, at the time of writing, is still standing. *Research by M. Hoddinott and R. Wilding.*

203

Spires

Look up to the rooftops to see some of Chester's spires. Many were planned, like Billy Hobby's Well, by John Douglas (1830-1911), who it was said was 'the doyen of provincial architects'. In partnership with Fordham until 1898 then Minshull, he designed a number of local buildings including the east side of St Werburgh Street.

Above: Chateau style houses in Bath Street 1903 Douglas and Minshull.

Overleaf, top left: North & South Wales Bank (now HSBC) 1883 Douglas and Fordham.

Overleaf, top right: Rectory of St John's (now Chester Visitor & Craft Centre) mid-18th century.

Overleaf, bottom left: Thimbleby's Tower (medieval) mock-14th century roof by Chester City Council Peter de Figueiredo.

Overleaf, bottom right: Cupola on the Bluecoat Hospital 1854.

The
tall world
lifts her gaze
To your painted windows sailing,
Shining gate to time's steep gallows,
Pulling hard the hissing seconds
With your iron limbs of tallest shadows.
A hollow room of sun and dark;
A hidden cavern deeply seething,
With Fleeting days   And gushing hours

Your girth   a coachman
Hunched   and lunging,
With dizzy   spires
Skyward   turning,
Your grinning   tower a   *Mike Penny*   silent jaw,
Down the   tumbling years
                                                gnawing.
To sudden   stars
Your lantern   calls,
Through rain and   drowsy evening shining
Your polished column   spears the winds
            Above the sulking city curling.

'At the end of a piece of thick white cord running from an
aperture at the base of the clock was a small white tassell,
as soon as the hour of 12.45 was reached (the hands having been
preset at that hour) the mayoress taking her time from Mr Joyce
(clockmaker) pulled the tassel and the Eastgate Clock started its
public career.'   Chronicle 27/5/1899

Clock designed   Inner workings
by Douglas &   by James Joyce
Minshull.   of Whitchurch.

205

The Eastgate Clock

The ornamental clock on the Eastgate is not Chester's only visible clock or even the oldest but it is the most famous. Its grand design was by Douglas and Minshull, local architects who, on behalf of the Duke of Westminster, came up with the first plans to improve the Eastgate in 1884. John Douglas's original plan was for a clock in stonework but it was agreed that this would contravene the law of 'ancient lights', blocking daylight to nearby properties.

By 1897 subscribers had donated money for several schemes to commemorate Queen Victoria's Jubilee. Colonel Edward Evans-Lloyd, a local solicitor, fed up with the length of time the project was taking, offered to pay for all the clock mechanism.

Winter time.

James Swindley, a cousin of Douglas and a blacksmith in Handbridge, accepted the commission for the intricate frame.

Inscription panels representing the emblems of England, Scotland, Wales and Ireland were made by the Coalbrookdale Iron Company.

Finally, by the 21st May 1899, the clock stood above the Eastgate. James Joyce of Whitchurch had made the inner workings – a pinwheel deadbeat system kept going by a pendulum weighing over a hundredweight (50k).

However the original idea had been to celebrate Queen Victoria's Jubilee but this had already taken place on 20th June 1897 with processions, flags and a 60 gun salute in the Castle yard. That evening two thousand pensioners had been treated to a 'meat tea' in the Town Hall and were given presents: 2 ounces of tobacco for the men, ½ pound of tea for the women. The River Dee had displayed 'God Save The Queen' banners on the shore, some illuminated by Chinese Lanterns and 'beautiful coloured miniature lights' on the suspension bridge whilst a floating convoy of steamers, barge and boats sailed past.

Statue of Queen Victoria at the Queen's School.

So, instead, the clock was set to start on Queen Victoria's 80th birthday on 27th May 1899. Until 1973 the firm of James Joyce wound the clock each week, then electric winding was introduced. In 1992 the whole mechanism was replaced by an electric one.

1891 It is claimed that the streets are not safe for respectable females on race days and therefore the races should be discontinued.
1892 Roodee enclosed during races. Admission charge – one shilling. £10,000 taken in 3 days. Porch attached to 'Anchorite Cell'.
1895 Fire destroys Dee Mills.
1897 Edward Langtree, husband of 'Jersey Lillie' (the King's mistress) dies in the County Lunatic Asylum, and is buried in Overleigh cemetery. He had fallen down steps on the Liverpool-Belfast steamboat and was found wandering along the railway at Crewe, and was 'committed'.

Nowadays visitors use over a tonne of paper each year for prints of the Eastgate Clock.

Collectables

Chemists' jars and pot lids for toothpaste and cold cream.

Before supermarkets and manufacturing conglomerates, containers were produced at a local level. Chemists had their own tubs, jars and bottles, pubs had their own beer and bottles, while mineral water companies, about eight in Chester, might sell water or 'pop' in their own branded bottles. Nowadays, water is the biggest selling 'soft drink' in the world.

RENDERS THE	VELVETINE CREAM	Top to bottom, left to right:
SKIN DELICATE	Prepared only by	DIRECTIONS
AND SOFT	JOHN SIMON	A little to be applied
PREVENTING	CHEMIST	to the hand and rubbed
ROUGHNESS		in until quite dry. The
IT IS NOT STICKY	4 Eastgate Row	most delicate needle
OR GREASY	CHESTER	work may be undertaken
		without washing the
		hands after using it

RICHMOND PHARMACY CHESTER   ROSE TOOTH PASTE

J.W. HUKE DISPENSARY 89 FOREGATE STREET CHESTER Superior Rose COLD CREAM

For Strengthening & Preserving the Teeth & Gums   CHERRY TOOTH PASTE
PREPARED BY CHEERS & HOPLEY CHEMISTS CHESTER

[Purple print] OZONIZED TOOTH PASTE   DSC REGISTERED TRADE MARK   PRICE 2S
FOR CLEANSING BEAUTIFYING AND PRESERVING THE TEETH & GUMS
PREPARED ONLY BY DAVIES & SHEPHEARD, CHEMISTS CHESTER

JOHN SIMON LATE J MILLS   Otto of Rose   COLD CREAM
CHEMIST   CHESTER
(Otto of Roses is said to have been discovered at the wedding feast of the
princess Nour-Djihan with the Emperor Djihaguyr, son of Akba when a moat
around the garden was filled with rose water. The sun's heat separated the
essential oil which rose to the surface and was skimmed off and found to
be a high quality perfume - produced in Persia from circa 1612.)

OTTO OF ROSE   COLD CREAM
G. KEMP   Chemist CHESTER

CHEERS & HOPLEY   HYGIENIC ARECA NUT
TOOTHPASTE   PURIFYING · CLEANSING
PREVENTS DECAY   CHESTER & BRANCHES

CHEERS & HOPLEY Superior COLD CREAM
6 NORTHGATE STREET   CHESTER

TOOTHPASTE for PRESERVING the TEETH & GUMS
RANDALL ROBERTS MPS   90 FOREGATE ST CHESTER

GEORGE W SHRUBSOLE
CHEMIST ESTD 1826 CHESTER
(The gap in the centre was for the addition of a
paper label which might explain the contents
and give a price.)

1897 Queen Victoria's Jubilee
has parade and 60 gun salute.
Dee illuminated for boat convoy.
1899 27th May Eastgate Clock started on
Queen's birthday. Mary Jonas, mother
of 33 children, dies.   Act for
Conservatory and Improvement of River
Dee. Electric streetlighting.
1900 City baths built by John Douglas.
1901 Green Cap School closed. Bollands
becomes a limited company.
1903 Electric trams. Statue of
Queen Victoria in castle square.
[Grey squirrels introduced to nearby Rossett]
1909 The Corn Exchange becomes the
Picture Drome (closed 1924).
1910 W.J. Lockwood designs St
Michael's Row. After an
outcry, tiled front top
is removed.

Chester bottles, left to right:

J W HUKE CHEMIST CHESTER   c 1910   standard square section aquaglass chemist's bottle

THE DEE MINERAL WATER CO LTD   CRYSTAL BREWED GINGER BEER 'D' TRADE MARK

      PORTLAND WORKS   CHESTER   c 1915   honey glaze stoneware crown top bottle

LAYCOCKS MINERAL WATER   Lion trademark   c 1915 aquaglass internal screw closure

WALKER & KNIGHT WINE & SPIRIT MERCHANTS NORTHGATE ST CHESTER   & stopper

      c 1900 stoneware two-tone dumpy ginger beer bottle

CHESTER MINERAL WATER CO LTD   phoenix trade mark c 1900 aquaglass codds bottle & marble
                                                                 enclosure

C CORDERY OLD NAG'S HEAD CHESTER   horse's head trademark

      c 1890   dark green blob top glass beer bottle

PARKER & CLEGG CHESTER   'P&C' trade mark

      c 1900   aquaglass codds bottle & marble enclosure

LAYCOCKS MINERAL WATER   Lion trademark

      c 1890s   blobtop aquaglass & bullet stopper

Front:

DONALD'S HAIR RESTORER THE CROSS CHESTER

      c 1910 cobalt blue glass

BUFFALO BILL'S

WILD WEST

COL. W. F. CODY

HISTORICAL SCENES

BUFFALO BILL'S

AMERICA'S NATIONAL ENTERTAINMENT.

AN ILLUSTRATED TREATISE OF HISTORICAL FACTS & SKETCHES.
PUBLISHED BY
BUFFALO BILL'S WILD WEST COMPANY.

COL. W. F. CODY (BUFFALO BILL), PRESIDENT.　　NATE SALSBURY, VICE-PRESIDENT & DIRECTOR.

JOHN M. BURKE ... ... General Manager	JULE KEEN ... ... Treasurer
ALBERT E. SHEIBLE ... ... Business Representative	LEW PARKER ... ...Contracting Agent
CARTER COUTURIER ... ... Advertising Agent	WILLIAM LANGAN ... ... Supply Agent

PROGRAMME.

OVERTURE - "Star Spangled Banner" - COWBOY BAND, WM. SWEENY, Leader

1.—**GRAND PROCESSIONAL REVIEW** and introduction of Groups and Individual Characters.

2.—**HORSE RACE** between a Cowboy, a Mexican and an Indian, on Spanish-Mexican Horses.

3.—**MISS ANNIE OAKLEY,** Celebrated Shot, who will illustrate her dexterity in the use of Fire-arms.

4.—**HISTORICAL ADVENTURE IN THE LIFE OF "BUFFALO BILL."** The famous Single Combat with "YELLOW HAND," Chief of the Sioux, at War Bonnet Creek, Dakota, and the downfall and death of the same on July 17th, 1875, in presence of the Indian and American Troops.

5.—**PONY EXPRESS.** The Former Pony Post Rider will show how the Letters and Telegrams of the Republic were distributed across the immense Continent previous to the Railways and the Telegraph.

6.—**ATTACK ON AN EMIGRANT TRAIN BY INDIANS, AND REPULSE BY THE COWBOYS.** At the conclusion of this Scene the "Virginia Reel" will be danced by Cowboys and the Prairie Girls on Horseback.
N.B.—The Waggons are the same as used 35 years ago.

7.—**JOHNNY BAKER,** Celebrated Young American Marksman.

8.—**COWBOY FUN.** Picking Objects from the Ground. Lassoing Wild Horses. Riding the Buckers.

9.—**PISTOL & REVOLVER SHOOTING.** Introduced by Mr. CLAUDE L. DALY.

10.—**RACING BETWEEN AMERICAN BACKWOODS WOMEN.**

11.—**CAPTURE OF THE DEADWOOD MAIL COACH BY THE INDIANS,** which will be rescued by "BUFFALO BILL" and his Attendant Cowboys.
N.B.—This is the identical old DEADWOOD COACH, called the Mail Coach, which is famous on account of having carried the great number of people who lost their lives on the road between DEADWOOD and Cheyenne 18 years ago. Now the most Famed Vehicle extant.

12.—**RACING BETWEEN INDIAN BOYS ON BAREBACK HORSES.**

13.—**LIFE CUSTOMS OF THE INDIANS.** Indian Settlement on the Field and "Path."

14.—**Col. W. F. CODY ("Buffalo Bill"),** in his Unique Feats in Sharpshooting.

15.—**BUFFALO HUNT,** as it is in the Far West of North America—"BUFFALO BILL" and Indians. The last of the only known Native Herd.

16.—**ATTACK ON A SETTLER'S CABIN**—Capture by the Indians—Rescue by "BUFFALO BILL" and the Cowboys.

17.—**SALUTE.**

NATIONAL ANTHEM.—CONCLUSION.

Buffalo Bill

In 1903 the balustrade of God's Providence House advertised Buffalo Bill's Wild West show. The spectacular event took place on the Roodee. William Cody (Buffalo Bill) was an American frontiersman with many claims to fame. Born in Iowa, he moved to Kansas where he learnt to ride and shoot, later becoming a pony express rider. He was employed as a wagon train guide and a hunter and served in the cavalry. In one season he killed 4,862 buffalos for meat to supply labourers building the Kansas Pacific railroad thus gaining his nickname. He was an expert scout, and killed the Cheyenne Chief Yellow Hand in hand-to-hand combat. His fame gained him a seat in the Nebraska Legislature but he soon resigned his 'desk job'. His European tours were an instant success, partly because he took along some of the native American 'Indians' who had the choice of staying in a reservation or travelling the world. While his show was in Britain one of the natives 'Black Hat' married a squaw at the Manchester Registry Office.

Buffalo Bill (4th from right) on the Roodee.

St Michael's Row

Edwardian Splendour

This Edwardian shopping arcade was built for the second Duke of Westminster by Chester architect W T Lockwood in 1911. The original baroque facade was replaced by timber framing after criticism, although white tiles can still be seen at street level.

The bandstand in winter.

Bandstand

The bandstand, a central feature on Chester's riverside groves, was built for £350. The mounted band of the Royal Artillery was the first band to play here on the 17ᵗʰ May 1913.

But whilst Edwardian Chester was enjoying the spring, tension in Europe was rising.

1911 Northgate Street Fire Station opens.

1913 Hydroelectricity produced on the Dee; Chester the first city to have it. Groves Bandstand open.

1917 Dee froze enough for skaters (also in 1929, 1947, 1963).

1921 Music Hall becomes cinema. Restriction on household coal to ½cwt a fortnight. Bakers offer to cook homemade meals at ½d per lb. Chester War Memorial built by Heswall & Sons. Chester butchers object to use of humane killer. Mass meeting of unemployed on Roodee. Pop: 40,802.

1923 Wireless listened to in Chester Cathedral Refectory. Louise Rayner (painter of Chester scenes) dies in Sussex.

LATEST ORDERS

OF THE

KAISER

TO HIS GENERALS.

It is my Royal and Imperial command that you concentrate your energies, for the immediate present, upon one single purpose, and that is that you address all your skill and all the valour of my **SOLDIERS to EXTERMINATE first, the treacherous English, walk over General French's contemptible little Army.**

Headquarters, Aix-la-Chapelle, August 19th, 1914.

What answer must Britons give ?

GOD SAVE THE KING.

These Posters may be purchased from S. G. MASON, Printer, 20, Frodsham Street, Chester.

S. G. MASON,

PRINTER & PUBLISHER.

TELEPHONE 545.

20, FRODSHAM STREET,

CHESTER.

Sept. 12th, 1914.

Dear Sir,

Enclosed is a specimen copy of the special Poster I have published showing the Kaiser's Orders to his Generals, and which has been referred to in the Press and correspondence as "the most effective Recruiting Poster." Orders have been received from a many Recruiting Officers, who all testify that the Posters have roused up a large number of Recruits. May I be favoured with an order for your district? A telephone message (545 Chester) will bring all particulars.

Yours truly,

S. G. MASON.

6, 1/6; 50, 8/6, 100, 15/-.

Post free.   Special prices for quantities.

REPRINTED FROM "DAILY DISPATCH" LONDON LETTER, September 11th, 1914.

The most effective Recruiting Bill.

"Our readers will not have forgotten the Kaiser's virulent address to his general officers, delivered at headquarters at Aix-la-Chapelle on August 19th, the text of which was subsequently revealed to this country by our contributor, Major Darnley Stuart-Stephens, through the Embassy of a friendly Power

"The Kaiser's reference to the British force, which has so successfully withstood and beaten back the *élite* of his generals and troops, although in a numerical inferiority of 1 to 4, has now been made the substance of recruiting bills and posters in Chester and elsewhere in this form: (here follows the wording on my poster)."

THESE POSTERS HAVE BEEN USED BY LORD ROBERTS, AND
THE FIRST LORD OF THE ADMIRALTY.

Poster and letter courtesy of Masons Design & Print, now at Viscount House, River Lane, Saltney.

RECRUITING

S.G. Mason served his apprenticeship at the Brook Street Steam Printing Works. He became a member of the Stationers' Company in 1903. At his first printing shop at 20 Frodsham Street in 1908 he started with an 'Arab' press which was used until the late 1950s. After expansion and several moves the company took a works in St John Street (now partly a cafe/bar) before resiting at Viscount House in Saltney.

1929 Stanley Palace given to city by Earl of Derby. Earl's Eye (The Meadows) given to city by Mayor Harry Brown. [Empire State Building started in New York.]

1931 Stairs from Frodsham Street to Walls erected at £288. Gaumont Palace Cinema opened.

1935 Odeon built (now listed building).

1937 Regal Cinema opens.

1938 First Lady Mayor, Mrs Phyllis Brown (of Browns of Chester). New Newgate built.

1939 [Frank Whittle builds first jet engine.]

1940 Chester's first civilian war casualty, Fireman Dutton.

1945 On VJ night a Bridge Street sewer collapses and a plague of rats heads for the Dee.

S.G. Mason's 'Arab' platen printing press. Based on a design originating in the United States it was built in Halifax by Josiah Wade Ltd and ran either from an overhead pulley or a foot treadle.

Britannia at Chester Castle during WWI.

Britannia

Before the year 1914
Birmingham Station was
being demolished. A
statue of Britannia with
the Norfolk Regimental
badge was sent to
Chester where they were
stationed. When the
regiment left the
Cheshire Regiment found
it useful for sharpening
bayonets.

Britannia at Chester Castle today.

myle ⁋ þan half þe þiknesse of þe erþe in
ward and doun rizt is þre þowsand tho hun
dred and fyue and fourty myle & somwhat
ouer as it were half a myle So zif helle is
in myddel of þe erþe doun rizt me nyzte knowe
howe meny myle is to helle De orbis dimisio
ne Augustin⁹ de ciuitate di li⁰. 16⁰. c⁰. 8⁰.

⁋ Ca. 6.   Or þe delynge of þe worlde take hede
þat þe grete see of Ocean byclyppeþ
al þe erþe aboute and þe erþe is ydeled
in þre grete parties ⁊ Asia is þat oon Europa
þat oþer and affrica þe pridde ⁋ But þese
þre parties beeþ not all euene ⁊ y liche mo
che · ffor Asia oon of þe þre conteyneþ half
þe erþe and strecþeþ from þe south by þe est

Extract from
John Trevissa's
15th century
translation
of the
Polychronicon.
Higden's
text here
was taken
from
Augustine.

NOWHERE NEAR PARADISE

Higden, in the Polychronicon (see page 61) gives the dimensions of the earth as
6491 miles (actually 7912). He then states (15th century translation) 'So if helle is in
[the] myddel of the erthe down rizt, me[n] myte knowe how many myle[s it is]
to helle.'

However there was, in 1355, 'a cellar in Brigge strete in breadth between the
cellar of William de Shavynton which is called Helle.'

The chartulary of the Hospital of St Anne (Harl. MS 2061) records 'a toft called
paradise' in 1426, but this was not the only part of Chester where
you might have wanted to live.

A deed of 1611/2 shows the messuage and lands in Handbridge commonly called Paradise. They are still there. Until a few years ago there was a Paradise Row opposite the racecourse, now a just a car parking place.

If these opposites don't fit the bill then a newspaper article of 30th August 1916 might sound interesting: 'At the Chester Police Court today a man named Harry Hand, whose address is 'nowhere'. Hand was ordered to pay 40s and handed over to the military authorities for being an absentee under the Military Services Act.'

When a famous pop group from Liverpool visited Chester they thought they were having the mickey taken when told about the unusual house name. After seeing for themselves they recorded the words, "He's a real Nowhere man, Living in his Nowhere land."

The late Ken Poole in his 'Tales of Chester' tells that, in 1980, the name was so sought after that, when a pair of semi-detached houses were built next to Nowhere, the new owners called their properties 1 and 2 Nowhere. The owner of Nowhere took them to court and the judge ruled that only he lived Nowhere; the two new houses were 1 and 2 River Lane.

There's nowhere on earth like it.

1948 Prince Charles, Prince of Wales, Earl of Chester, born.
1949 Blue Coat School closes.
1951 Mystery Plays performed after gap of nearly 4 centuries. Food at Chester Hospital said to be 'disgraceful'. Upton counterfeit coiner gets 7 years.
1961 Population 58,950.
1963 [President J.F.Kennedy assassinated, news flash in Britain.]
1966 Queen Elizabeth II visits Chester Races.
1967 Public market closes for demolition.
1969 Northgate Brewery closes.

1971 St Anne Fire Station opens
1979 Father John Plessington is canonised.
        (see 1679)

Rebus

When Dean Bennet had a series of stained-glass windows installed in the cloisters of Chester Cathedral during 1920 he had to find sponsors. So for each of the saints on their saint days, scholars, kings, gospel-writers as well as Earl Hugh and Ranulph Higden, a donor is recorded on each window. The dean also left his own name but this is harder to find as it is hidden in a rebus: a picture puzzle representing words.

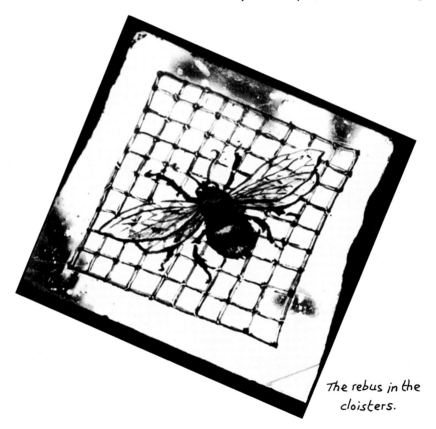

The rebus in the cloisters.

In St Peter's Church a palindrome can be found in the oak canopy of the font. The Greek NIYON ANOMHMA MH MONAN OYIN translates as 'I wash away my sins, not my face alone.' It is only the Greek inscription which is spelt the same from both ends.

SUSPENSION

The first suspension bridge to Queen's Park was built by the contractor James Dredge in 1852 and was private.

It was replaced, in 1923, by an 84·4 metre bridge erected by David Rowell & Co.

Shields of the city's seven Norman earls decorate the towers of this well-known landmark.

1972 Chester Team Parish formed.
1973 First blue plaque erected by council. Prince Charles given freedom of city.
1974 The city and rural districts join under one authority. Chester Poets publish first anthology.
1975 City arms altered to adjust for new area. 1580 motto is kept, the badge is altered and castle pendants added for castles at Shotwick and Beeston. The crest is entwined with oak to show additional country areas. George Pace's Addleshaw Tower built to hold the cathedral bells, the first separate bell tower built since the Middle Ages.

WESTERN COMMAND

Under George V, Watergate House was used as the Western Command HQ but by 1938 a new HQ had been built beside the river in Handbridge.

Edward VIII only reigned for 325 days. He abdicated after strong opposition to his proposed marriage to Wallis Simpson (Mrs Wallis Warfield), a divorcee. Given the title Duke of Windsor, he married in France during June 1937.

The Western Command Headquarters in Handbridge was built by the War Office Directorate of Fortifications and Works. During World War II its underground network of shelters, war rooms and escape tunnels to the river (now bricked up) were linked to other offices by the Defence Telephone Network with one line on land and another across the Dee. It has been suggested that the ER on the gates stand for Edward Rex but the main entrance (now preserved inside the new building) has the letters GR: George VI had succeeded his brother by the time the building opened. The HQ's drab appearance led Pevsner and Hubbard, writing in the 'Buildings of England, Cheshire' to describe it as 'a nonentity'. Recently the buildings have been given a new lease of life. The mock-Roman temple now dominating the riverside is, perhaps, dedicated to the god, Capital.

ER (Elizabeth Regina and not Edward, according to local historian Len Morgan) on the Western Command HQ gates (now the Capital Bank).

224

EWS

During World War II 'Emergency Water Supplies' had to be arranged in case of fires. Huge water tanks (there were some in the Cathedral grounds) supplied large pipes set against the street gutters. All wardens' posts had stirrup pumps and buckets to deal with fires and, to help the blackout and save confusion, no bonfires were to be lit in November.

The headquarters of the Civil Defence was under the town hall in the old police station (later Chester Record Office), where large posts shored up the ceiling in case of bombing damage. In the appendix to Weekly Order No 78 it is stated: 'In air attacks on this country the enemy has been including a certain proportion of incendiary bombs containing an explosive charge. When this type of bomb explodes it scatters molten magnesium and steel splinters for considerable distances... Whilst burning these bombs behave in the same way as normal incendiary bombs...' Information followed on making shields to tackle bombs which landed on premises likely to catch fire. Otherwise it was recommended that sandbags be placed on the bomb in open areas.

Although the city did not suffer from large scale bombing there were some attacks. There were bomb shelters at The Blossoms, St Michael's Row, in the vaults of Oddfellows Hall and the crypt of St John's Church. Fireman Cyril George Dutton was Chester's first civilian casualty of the war. He was killed by falling rubble at the rear of Foregate Street on 29th November 1940. Of five civilian casualties in the city, two were firemen.

EWS sign at the old Bowling Green (now the Catholic club) in Brook Street.

FIREFIGHTERS

Northgate Street Fire Station of 1846
CRO 942·714 BAT

1086 The Domesday Book records that if a fire burnt the city the person responsible was fined three pence and had to pay his neighbour two shillings.

1140 Fire destroys a large part of the city. (In the same century York was virtually destroyed)

1180 Parading St Werburgh's shrine through the streets is said to have prevented a great fire.

1278 Another great fire sweeps the city.

1494 A great fire destroys much of Northgate Street.

1564 and 5 Fires destroy Northgate Street and Handbridge.

1569 Chester Assembly orders 'For the better Savegarde of the Said citie from danger of ffyer … before Easter … every Alderman … shall have in redines four bucketts … and every common counsaile … one buckett'.

1591 A hook with rings (for pulling down buildings) is added to the city's fire equipment.

1709 The first volunteer fire brigade is formed and a fire engine house built for five hand-operated pumps. Despite a petition from the Bakers they are not allowed to stack more than 30 kids of gorse or faggots (bundles of sticks) in any building. Flaxdressers and Ostlers are banned from smoking at work or using open candles.

1761 A new fire engine house is built.

1762 Thirty firemen live within the city.

1803 The police force act as the fire brigade.

1846 A fire station is built in Northgate Street.

1853 The firemen/policemen resign (as firemen) as the work is too onerous.

1862 The exchange (town hall) burns down.

1863 The City of Chester Volunteer Fire Brigade is formed, with seven officers and sixty men. Any member heard to curse, swear or use any blasphemous expression on duty is fined 5s.

Northgate Street Fire Station of 1911

1870 A new fire engine house is built at the Potato Market in Northgate Street to house a horse-drawn manual engine, a wheeled ladder and a hand-drawn manual engine.

1895 Merryweather horse-drawn steam fire engine bought.

1911 Northgate Street Fire Station costing £3,000 opens.

1920, 29, 34, 39 Dennis Brothers' fire engines are bought.

1938 Morris turntable ladder is bought.

1940 Fireman C G Dutton killed by falling timbers after the 20th November air raid.

1941 The Fire Service is nationalised.

1948 The brigade reforms as City of Chester Fire Services.

1971 The new St Anne Street Fire Station opens.

Morris 85' Turntable Ladder

Firemark or Fire Sign issued by the Sun Assurance Company.

There are Fire Signs in Castle Street, Lower Bridge Street and Abbey Street. This one is in Handbridge.

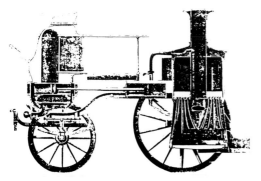

Merryweather Steam Fire Engine

Sign at the Pied Bull.

Signs of the times

Before star and crown ratings, came the triangle of the Road and Path Cycling Association who recommended hotels and guest houses early in the 20th century. Nowadays cycling storage can be found all around the city.

The Crown and Glove sign in Easgate Street is from a former pub. The symbol refers to the time when a monarch could be challenged on his accession.

After having his lunch break and a few pints at the Marlborough Arms in the early 1990's, the signwriter repeated his earlier letters. Many people went into the pub to tell the landlord of the mistake so that, realising it was good for business, the new sign was produced with the earlier hand-painted error!

Crown & Glove

228

The 'Marlbororough' Arms

A motley crew

Raft Race

With its yearly theme, colourful costumes, a variety of craft and dirty tactics – including sabotage, firing paint, water and fish remains – it is a wonder that anyone wins.

However, it's all for fun and for local charities. The annual spring raft race is organised by Chester Rotary Club and funded by entry fees and space sold for the event on the meadows.

The crew with the best interpretation of the year's theme is awarded a prize by the Admiral of the Dee (see page 66).

1975 St Michael's Church becomes Heritage Centre. St Mary-on-the-hill purchased by Cheshire C.C.

1984 Library built in Westminster Works.

1985 Roodee 'County Stand' burns down.

1991 Deva Mosaic built under direction of Russell Kirk by 60 children from Chester District primary schools.

1992 The queen makes Mrs Sue Proctor Chester's first Lord Mayor. 'A Celebration of Chester' bronze statue unveiled.

1995 Rufus Court built.

1997 Christine Russell is elected the first female and first Labour MP for the city. Cheshire Regiment Garden of Remembrance redesigned to represent a medal and ribbon.

ADDLESHAW TOWER

Built in 1975 and designed by George Pace for Dean Addleshaw, the Cathedral bell-tower was the first free-standing belltower built in Europe since the Middle Ages.

It contains 13 bells, some dating from the 17th century. The curfew bell however, is still in the Cathedral tower.

Garden of Remembrance

Medal

The Garden of Remembrance is for soldiers who fought in the Second World War. A book of names for those who died, serving in the 22nd Cheshire Regiment, can be found in the Cathedral. The garden was redesigned in 1997 to represent a medal and ribbon, best seen from the city wall.

Victorian *Street*
Chester Visitor Centre

Chester Resculptured

An attempt to recreate Chester's rows from Victorian times has been made in the Chester Visitor Centre where a mock street complete with a fully-stocked chemist's shop and other period wares can be seen.

At the Grosvenor Museum is a Period House with Victorian, Georgian and Stuart rooms. (Not shown)

1997 Top Coes is third horse to win the Chester Cup twice this century. New nave floor in cathedral. Chester citizens leave floral tributes to the Late Countess of Chester – Diana, Princess of Wales – outside the Town Hall.

1998 Flagpoles erected outside the Forum and the Town Hall. Quakers protest against the bombing of Baghdad, at the Cross. Eastgate Street repaved. Tarmac and lights on towpath. Models of Chester buildings put on exhibition in Bridge Street Row. Medieval road found on Infirmary site.

1999 Bridge Street repaved. Chester Archaeological Society celebrate 150th anniversary. Boat shaped scout hut built in Old Port.

Eastgate Street

When Fiona Richards created a model of a Chester building as a student she had no idea that she would go on to make clay copies of nearly all the buildings in the city centre complete with rooftops, chimneys and shopfronts.

With 'Paper Clay Designs' she has gone on to produce copied architecture in clay mounted on watercolour backgrounds.

Her exhibition is currently in The Rather Nice Card Shop (Saint Michael's Rectory) on Bridge Street Row East.

Models from:
  Paper Clay Designs
  The Granary
  Henley
  Near Ludlow
  Shropshire
  01584 876224

The corner of the 'modern' Shoemakers' Row

Garden for the Blind statue.

Ymir

With the sun and moon as breasts and a serpent on his arm, Ymir, the source of the world can be found depicted in Grosvenor Park. Carved from Portland Stone by Phillip Bews, the statue was commissioned by Chester Civic Trust in Cheshire Celebration Year, 1993, and unveiled by His Grace the Duke of Westminster in the Garden for the Blind.

In Norse and Germanic mythology, Ymir was the first living creature formed with fire and ice from chaos. He was nourished by his cow companion, Audhumia. The next beings were created from his sweat.

Slain by Odin, Vili and Ve — Ymir's carcass became the base of the world. His blood became the seas, his flesh the land, his bones the mountains, his teeth shingle on the shore.

Ymir's skull formed the heavens and his brains the clouds. Sparks caught in the skull created the sun, moon and stars.

DEVA

A mosaic in Roman style looks up from the Roman Gardens at the city wall. Designed partly by Russell Kirk, a local artist, the pieces were put together by sixty primary school children from Cheshire schools. The idea of a gorgon's head with snakes for hair was taken from a stone in the gallery at the Grosvenor Museum. Doves who were supporting a Roman lady called Curatia are taken from another gravestone there, and dolphins also appear.

The Deva mosaic in the Roman Gardens.

POSTSCRIPT Information on nearly all aspects covered in this book can be found in the Chester Collection (contact Chester Record Office at the Town Hall or Cheshire Record Office in Duke Street) or in Chester Reference Library. Queries directed to the author should include a SAE.

INDEX

Floating swimming baths on the River Dee C19th

Ornamental iron posts found in a line through Boughton, on the end of the Old Dee Bridge, in Edgar's Field and through Curzon Park are Victorian sewer vents.

Seal of St Mary's Nunnery
(see page 84)

Shoemakers' Row, Northgate Street   Late C19th

The remaining arch of
the old Market Hall.

Cathedral Boiler.

OTHER BOOKS PUBLISHED BY GORDON EMERY

CHESTER *Inside Out*   Gordon Emery   (Hardback Limited Edition of 500) £12-95
MILLER OF DEE   Roy Wilding   £9-99
HIDDEN HIGHWAYS OF CHESHIRE   R J A Dutton   £9-99
CURIOUS CLWYD   Gordon Emery   £11-99
CURIOUS CLWYD 2   Gordon Emery   £11-99
HIDDEN HIGHWAYS OF NORTH WALES R J A Dutton £9-99
GUIDE TO THE MAELOR WAY   £6-95
WALKS SERIES 99p each (Send SAE for full List)

AVAILABLE AT ALL GOOD BOOKSHOPS OR BY POST (Add £1-00 post + packing)
FROM GORDON EMERY, 27 GLADSTONE ROAD, CHESTER CH1 4BZ